PRENTICE HALL
LITERATURE

PENGUIN  EDITION

General Resources

Grade Twelve

PEARSON
Prentice
Hall

Upper Saddle River, New Jersey
Boston, Massachusetts

ISBN 0-13-165319-9

1 2 3 4 5 6 7 8 9 10   09 08 07 06 05

Contents

PROFESSIONAL DEVELOPMENT 1

Differentiated Instruction 2

Vocabulary Knowledge Rating 4

Vocabulary Knowledge Rating Chart 5

Introducing Expressive Vocabulary 6

Anticipation Guide 8

Anticipation Guide Form 10

KWL 11

KWL Chart 12

Vocab-o-Gram 13

Vocab-o-Gram Chart 14

Word Forms 15

Word Form Chart 16

Response Journals 17

Response Journal Starters 19

Two-Column Response Journal 20

Literature Circles 21

Roles in Literature Circles 23

Save the Last Word for Me 24

Save the Last Word for Me Response Page 26

ReQuest (Reciprocal Questioning) 27

Question-Answer Relationships (QAR) 28

Reading Log 29

Reading Log, Student Page 30

Interpretation Chart 31

Interpretation Chart, Student Page 32

Paired Discussion 33

Paired Discussion, Student Page 34

Think-Pair-Share 35

Think-Pair-Share, Student Page 36

Give One, Get One 37

Give One, Get One, Student Page 38

Discussion Guide 39

**WRITING RUBRICS FOR SELF-ASSESSMENT
LISTENING AND SPEAKING RUBRICS** 41

Autobiographical Narrative *4-point, 5-point* 43

Autobiographical Narrative *6-point* 44

Persuasive Essay *4-point, 5-point* 45

Persuasive Essay   *6-point* 46
Reflective Essay   *4-point, 5-point* 47
Reflective Essay   *6-point* 48
Job Portfolio   *4-point, 5-point* 49
Job Portfolio   *6-point* 50
Research Paper   *4-point, 5-point* 51
Research Paper   *6-point* 52
Multimedia Report   *4-point, 5-point* 53
Multimedia Report   *6-point* 54
Cause-and-Effect Essay   *4-point, 5-point* 55
Cause-and-Effect Essay   *6-point* 56
Short Story   *4-point, 5-point* 57
Short Story   *6-point* 58
Problem-and-Solution Essay   *4-point, 5-point* 59
Problem-and-Solution Essay   *6-point* 60
Business Letter   *4-point, 5-point* 61
Business Letter   *6-point* 62
Descriptive Essay   *4-point, 5-point* 63
Descriptive Essay   *6-point* 64
Response to Literature   *4-point, 5-point* 65
Response to Literature   *6-point* 66
Writing for Assessment   *4-point, 5-point* 67
Writing for Assessment   *6-point* 68
Comparison-and-Contrast Essay   *4-point, 5-point* 69
Comparison-and-Contrast Essay   *6-point* 70
Summary   *4-point, 5-point* 71
Summary   *6-point* 72
Poem   *4-point, 5-point* 73
Poem   *6-point* 74
Critique   *4-point, 5-point* 75
Critique   *6-point* 76
Biographical Essay   *4-point, 5-point* 77
Biographical Essay   *6-point* 78
Reader Response Journal   *4-point, 5-point* 79
Reader Response Journal   *6-point* 80
Generic (Holistic) Writing Rubric   *4-point, 5-point* 81
Generic (Holistic) Writing Rubric   *6-point* 82
Listening: Analyzing Persuasive Techniques 83
Listening: Critiquing Persuasive Arguments 84

General Resources

Listening: Analyzing Advertising 85

Listening: Media Analysis of the News 86

Listening and Speaking: Interview Techniques 87

Speaking: Delivering an Autobiographical Presentation 88

Speaking: Delivering a Persuasive Speech 89

Speaking: Presenting an Oral Response to Literature 90

Speaking: Presenting a Proposal 91

Speaking: Delivering a Research Presentation 92

ALTERNATIVE ASSESSMENT MATERIALS 93

Reading Strategy Inventory 95

Preparing to Read 98

Independent Reading Guide: The Novel 100

Independent Reading Guide: The Short Story .102

Independent Reading Guide: The Play 104

Independent Reading Guide: Nonfiction 106

Independent Reading Guide: Poetry 108

Independent Reading Guide: Myths and Folk Tales 110

Initial Self-Assessment: Writing 112

Peer Conferencing Notes: Reader 114

Proofreading Checklist 116

Writing Self-Assessment 118

Portfolio Planner 120

Portfolio Record 122

Portfolio Final Self-Evaluation 124

Portfolio Final Evaluation: Teacher Rating 125

Self-Assessment: Speech 127

Peer Assessment: Speech 128

Peer Assessment: Oral Interpretation 129

Peer Assessment: Dramatic Performance 130

Self-Assessment: Listening 131

Self-Assessment: Speaking and Listening Progress 132

Speaking Progress Chart: Teacher Observation 133

Teacher Observation Checklist 134

Home Parent Letter 137

Self-Assessment Home Review 138

Homework Log 139

Writing: Home Review Letter 140

Listening: Analyzing Advertising ....
Listening: Media Analysis of the News ....
Listening and Speaking: Interview Techniques ....
Speaking: Delivering an Autobiographical Presentation ....
Speaking: Delivering a Persuasive Speech ....
Speaking: Presenting an Oral Response to Literature ....
Speaking: Presenting a Proposal ....
Speaking: Delivering a Research Presentation ....

ALTERNATIVE ASSESSMENT MATERIALS

Reading Strategy Inventory ....
Preparing to Read ....
Independent Reading Guide: The Novel ....
Independent Reading Guide: The Short Story ....
Independent Reading Guide: The Play ....
Independent Reading Guide: Nonfiction ....
Independent Reading Guide: Poetry ....
Independent Reading Guide: Myths and Folk Tales ....
Initial Self-Assessment: Writing ....
Peer Conferencing: Notes Reader ....
Proofreading Checklist ....
Writing Self-Assessment ....
Portfolio Planner ....
Portfolio Record ....
Portfolio Final Self-Evaluation ....
Portfolio Final Evaluation: Teacher Rating ....
Self-Assessment: Speech ....
Peer Assessment: Speech ....
Peer Assessment: Oral Interpretation ....
Peer Assessment: Dramatic Performance ....
Self-Assessment: Listening ....
Self-Assessment: Speaking and Listening Progress ....
Speaking Progress Chart: Teacher Observation ....
Teacher Observation Checklist ....
Home Enrichment Letter ....
Self-Assessment: Home Review ....
Homework Log ....
Writing: Home Review Letter ....

Professional Development

Differentiated Instruction

Description

The wide range of academic diversity found in schools today presents both a challenge and an opportunity to all teachers. The goal of a comprehensive language arts program remains the provision of universal access for all students to an intellectually rich and challenging language arts curriculum and instruction in addition to whatever specialized intervention may be required.

Universal access occurs when teachers provide curriculum and instruction in ways that allow all learners in the classroom to participate and to achieve the instructional and behavioral goals of general education and the core curriculum. Teachers will succeed in providing universal access if they teach in heterogeneous, inclusive classrooms and consistently and systematically integrate instructional strategies that are responsive to the needs of typical learners, gifted learners, less proficient readers, English language learners, and students who are eligible for and receiving special education services.

Strategies

The following is a basic list of instructional considerations that can be applied across all phases of instruction.

- **Clarify behavioral expectations** for the lesson. Students need to understand the parameters within which they are working.

- **Provide time for students to collect their thoughts** before having to speak. You may want to ask a student a question and then pause before you assist the student in responding. You may also want to ask the student a question, state that you want the student to think about it, and indicate that you will be back for the response in a minute. Another possibility is to tell students the questions that you will be asking during tomorrow's class in order to give them time, overnight, to prepare their responses. These suggestions can be very helpful for a student experiencing a language disability or for a student who uses an alternative, augmentative communication device.

- **Use visuals throughout the lesson.** Outlining key ideas, writing key phrases and vocabulary on the overhead projector or board, or putting notes on the overhead projector or board are critical supports for many students. You may want to provide some students with a copy of your overheads or notes ahead of time so that they can follow along. For other students, make a partial or blank copy of the graphic or outline you will be using and require students to write in key information as it is discussed. It is very helpful if you model this filling-in procedure for students. It also helps them to overcome problems with spelling or capturing complex ideas using only a few words.

- **Schedule opportunities for preteaching and reteaching** key concepts, vocabulary words, and skills. Students will most likely need more than one opportunity to gain understanding and fluency.

- **Assist in time management.** When requiring students to complete projects or long-term assignments, provide a calendar that breaks down the requirements by due dates. Go over the checklist with the students and monitor their use of the checklist and task completion as the assignment proceeds. Many students will experience significant difficulties in self-managing the time needed to complete complex and long-term assignments.

- **Consider alternative means for demonstrating understanding.** Think beyond the common modes of reading and writing. Students could present information orally, create a poster or visual representation of a work, tape-record their ideas, or act out their understanding. These activities take into consideration multiple intelligences and can provide access for all learners in the classroom.

- **Have students begin all work in class.** Prior to class dismissal, check to ensure that each student has a good start and understands what is expected.

- **Build vocabulary** by teaching the meaning of prefixes and suffixes. Also, focus on synonyms and antonyms of words and have students define the words in their own words.

- **Explicitly teach note-taking skills.** Model note-taking as you present information to the classroom. Collect and review the students' notes and provide suggestions for improvement.

- **Use recorded readings.** Some students can benefit from the use of books on tape/CD. Be sure that students are actively engaged and following along as they listen to the tape/CD.

- **Balance student-focused and directed activities with teacher-focused and directed activities.** Students who are less proficient readers, English language learners, and students with disabilities will often require explicit instruction and modeling. Student-focused activities may assist students in gaining numerous skills, but they need to be balanced with teacher-directed lessons that provide explicit instruction by the teacher. Clearly stating expectations, modeling what students are to do, providing examples of finished projects, and explicitly teaching vocabulary words, reading comprehension strategies, and strategies for approaching text in a strategic, active way are necessary for these students' success. Other students can benefit from this explicitness of instruction as well. Being explicit does not mean watering down or dumbing down the curriculum; it means making it explicit so that all students can access it.

Vocabulary Knowledge Rating

Description

Vocabulary Knowledge Rating is a strategy for assessing students' familiarity with important terms in a reading selection by having them independently rate how well they know these terms. This preassessment enables you to get a realistic gauge of students' expressive and receptive vocabulary knowledge—that is, words they actually understand versus words they simply recognize. You are then able to provide focused and substantive preteaching as necessary.

Steps

1. List the Vocabulary Builder words and expressive vocabulary for a given selection on a Vocabulary Knowledge Rating Chart and distribute copies of it. When students have the list, tell them that they will prepare for reading the new selection by assessing what they already know about important vocabulary in it.

2. Pronounce each word as students complete the knowledge-rating process so that decoding is not a problem. As you read each word aloud, ask students to rate their word knowledge by checking one of the columns on the chart:

   1 = Know it: I know this word well (can define it and use it in an intelligent sentence).
   2 = Kind of know it: I have heard or seen this word (but not sure what it means).
   3 = Do not know it: I have not seen or heard the word before.

   Remind students not to indicate that they *know* a word (Rating 1) if they simply *recognize* a word (Rating 2). Also encourage them not to hesitate to indicate that they do not recognize or understand a word at all (Rating 3). Invite them to be honest, as you will use their input to decide what words you will preteach and discuss.

3. Use the ratings for a unified-class discussion. Tally how many students actually know (or think they know) each word and encourage them to share their knowledge. In this way, you will be able to gauge just how much prereading instruction you need to provide. Follow up this assessment and brainstorming process with focused instruction of terms that are totally unfamiliar, somewhat familiar, or clearly misunderstood.

4. Draw students' attention to the Vocabulary Builder notations in the side columns of their textbook. Point out that the words are placed to provide them with a meaning in the context of the reading. They should apply the meanings as they read.

5. After you have completed instruction and students have read the assigned selection, have them return to their Vocabulary Knowledge Rating Charts and re-rate themselves. Then, return to the selection or use reference books to clarify words that are still problematic.

6. Let students know that this Vocabulary Knowledge Rating Chart is an organizer for study. Any words on the list may appear on the Selection Test. Students should also be held accountable for using these terms in related oral or written work.

Source

Blachowicz, C., and Fisher, P.J. (2002). *Teaching Vocabulary in All Classrooms*. Upper Saddle River, NJ: Merrill/Prentice Hall.

Name _____ Class _____ Date _____

Vocabulary Knowledge Rating Chart

Directions: As your teacher reads the words, think about what each word might mean and mark the appropriate number in the Before Reading column.

    ① = Know it   ② = Kind of know it   ③ = Do not know it

After you have read and discussed the selection, rate the words again in the After Reading column. Then, write definitions and examples or sentences to help you clarify and remember the words.

Selection _____

Word	Rating		Definition	Example/Sentence
	Before Reading	After Reading		

Introducing Expressive Vocabulary

Background

Vocabulary is the term we use to describe the total number of words and phrases an individual understands at some level. Language researchers often describe vocabulary being further subdivided into receptive vocabulary, which are words understood from listening or reading, and expressive vocabulary, which are words communicated by speaking or writing. Receptive or passive vocabulary is typically far larger than expressive vocabulary, including many words that are at least partially understood but not fully integrated into one's expressive vocabulary. To succeed academically, students need to not only recognize a wide array of specialized terminology, but also comfortably utilize sophisticated vocabulary in both oral and written contexts.

Instructional Implications

Research suggests that the comprehensive development of academic vocabulary, the particular terms used primarily in academic settings, requires directly teaching new terms (receptive vocabulary) and structured tasks that require students to apply newly acquired words in discussion and writing to build their expressive vocabulary. Unfortunately, simply listening to articulate language used by a teacher or encountering novel terms in a reading selection will not automatically transfer to confident and competent student application. Practical guidelines for introducing new terms as well as fostering expressive vocabulary development via structured discussion and writing tasks are provided in the following sections.

Steps to Teach a New Term

1. **Pronounce the word and clarify the part of speech.**
   This article focuses on an <u>ecstatic</u> *moment in a high school student's life.*
   Ecstatic is an adjective, a word used to describe.

2. **Ask students to all repeat the word once or twice.**
   Say the word <u>ecstatic</u> *with me. (ec stat' ic)*

3. **Explain—provide an accessible synonym and/or a brief explanation.**
   <u>*Ecstatic*</u> *means extremely happy.*

4. **Elaborate—make connections (image, descriptive sentence, etc.).**
   Showing image: a picture of a soccer team receiving the championship trophy.
   Showing sentence: I was <u>ecstatic</u> when our team won the soccer championship.

5. **Assess—Ask focused questions to see if students seem to grasp the word's meaning (vs. Any questions? Do you understand? Is that clear?).**
   Would you be ecstatic if you won the lottery?
   Would you be ecstatic if you were assigned a 20-page report to complete over Spring break?

Steps to Structuring the Expressive Use of a New Term

Simply telling students to use newly taught words in discussion and writing activities is not likely to significantly enhance expressive vocabulary. Students will be far more likely to independently use a richer variety of academic language if they have had the benefit of initial structured classroom application tasks.

Structured Oral Applications via Guided Writing and Discussion

Discussion:

1. **Review the target word.**
   "One of our target academic terms that means exceptionally happy is _____."
   (that is correct, ecstatic)

2. **Model the appropriate use of the new term in a complete sentence (with appropriate syntax and grammar).**
   "I was ecstatic to hear our team had won the championship."
   "I was ecstatic when I learned that our team had won the championship."

3. **Provide one or more sentence starters for students to complete individually**
   "I was ecstatic when_____."
   "I was ecstatic to_____."

4. **Partner rehearsal:** Students take turns sharing their examples using complete sentences including the target word.

5. **Class discussion:** Structured sharing of relevant examples, provide feedback and remodeling as necessary.

Writing:

Linguistic scaffolds such as sentence starters or paragraph frames are particularly helpful for less proficient writers; however, they are not meant to be straitjackets for students capable of more creative and autonomous application. Without structured applications, students most in need of developing academic discourse skills are apt to flounder, producing poorly constructed written products comprised largely of everyday spoken English.

1. **Design a task that warrants the application of the new vocabulary.**
   For example, sentences, paragraphs, and essays.
   #### Sentence Level
   Provide relevant sentence starters that model the appropriate use of the word as well as sentence structure (syntax and grammar).
   "I was ecstatic (base form of verb: e.g., to learn that_____, to receive_____, when I + verb/past tense)."
   #### Paragraph/Essay Level
   Provide a relevant sentence starter for each of the suggested terms.
   Provide a relevant paragraph frame including a topic sentence, transitional expressions, and target vocabulary.

2. **Assessment rubric**
   Use of target vocabulary is identified.
   For example, "The writer appropriately applies 4–6 new lesson terms."

Anticipation Guide

Description

A productive way to assess students' familiarity with a topic or concept and to motivate active and purposeful reading is to use an Anticipation Guide. The Anticipation Guide, initially developed by Herber (1978), enhances students' reading comprehension by activating their background knowledge and experiences, focusing their attention on the important concepts or big ideas addressed in the selection, and encourages them to react to specific ideas in the text. This strategy is appropriate for both narrative and informational texts.

Students react to thought-provoking statements on the Anticipation Guide before they read. An important element of strategy is the discussion that takes place after students independently respond to the statements. This prereading discussion of responses elicits relevant background knowledge, preconceived ideas, and any possible misconceptions. Because the Anticipation Guide revolves around the reading selection's most important concepts, students are motivated to pay close attention to this information while reading.

After reading the selection, students return to their prereading responses to see if the text actually supports their initial responses. You may have students identify evidence to support their postreading responses to the Anticipation Guide statements. When students have completed their reading and revisited their initial responses, you may use the Anticipation Guide to anchor the postreading discussion, enabling you to evaluate how well students have understood the material and to make sure that misconceptions have been corrected.

Steps

1. Using the form provided, create an Anticipation Guide for the selection students will read. You may insert the statements provided in the Motivation note in the Annotated Teacher's Edition, add further statements, or create your own statements.

   These statements should address key points, major concepts, and broad—possibly controversial—ideas students will encounter in the selection, rather than specific supporting details. They should be worded to provoke agreement or disagreement. The most effective statements are those about which students have some knowledge but do not necessarily have a complete or mature understanding. If appropriate, you might also include one or two statements that are likely to tap into glaring misconceptions about the topic. You might also consider planting a few important words from the selection or expressive vocabulary within your statements so that you have a focused opportunity to address them.

2. Copy the Anticipation Guide and distribute it to students. Read aloud each statement on the Anticipation Guide and clarify any potentially unfamiliar vocabulary. Tell students to react to each statement quietly and independently, formulate a response to it, and be prepared to defend their opinions.

3. If the ideas are fairly complex, place students with a partner or in small groups to discuss their reactions before debriefing as a unified class. They may indicate their consensus as a group in the "Group" column.

4. Engage the unified class in a prereading discussion by reading each statement aloud and then asking for a hand count (or thumbs up or down) of responses. Call on students from each side of the issue to justify their responses. Refrain from telling them the correct response, thereby negating any incentive to actually read the text.

5. Have students read the selection, with the purpose of finding evidence that confirms, rejects, or elaborates on each of the statements in the Anticipation Guide.

6. After students finish reading, have them return to the statements to determine whether they have changed their minds regarding any of the presented ideas. Either independently or in small groups, have them locate the information from the text that supports or disproves each statement. Students may then rewrite any statement that needs to be altered based on what they have read.

7. Lead a unified class discussion of what students have learned from the reading, tackling one statement at a time and asking students first to share relevant information from the text and then their revision (if necessary) of the original statement.

Sources

Buehl, D. (2001). *Classroom Strategies for Interactive Learning.* Newark, DE: International Reading Association.

Herber, H. (1978). *Teaching Reading in Content Areas,* 2nd ed. Upper Saddle River, NJ: Prentice Hall.

Readence, J.E., Bean, T.W., and Baldwin, R.S. (1995). *Content Area Reading: An Integrated Approach,* 5th ed. Dubuque, IA: Kendall/Hunt.

Wood, K.D. (2001). *Literacy Strategies Across the Subject Areas: Process-Oriented Blackline Masters for the K-12 Classroom.* Boston: Allyn and Bacon.

Name _____ Class_____ Date _____

Anticipation Guide Form

Directions: Before reading, mark in the Me column whether you agree (A) or disagree (D) with each statement. Be prepared to support your opinions with specific reasons and examples from your prior knowledge and experiences. Then, discuss your responses with your group and mark the group's decision in the Group column. As you read, look for information or details that support your opinion or cause you to change your mind. After reading, mark whether you still agree or disagree.

Selection _____

Before Reading		Statements	After Reading
Me	Group		
		1.	
		2.	
		3.	
		4.	
		5.	
		6.	
		7.	
		8.	

KWL

Description

KWL is a strategy that models the active thinking needed when getting ready to read and actually reading to learn from expository text. The letters *K*, *W*, and *L* stand for three activities students engage in when reading to learn: recalling what they *Know* (activating prior knowledge), determining what they *Want* to learn (setting a purpose for reading), and identifying what they *Learn* as they read (recalling and summarizing). It is a particularly useful strategy to apply to expository or informational texts. It is very important to scaffold the use of KWL with students. Do not just hand them the chart and expect them to use it on their own. Guide them through each phase of the process.

Steps

1. Engage students in a brainstorming session about what they as a group already know about the concept or the topic of the reading. Be aware that underprepared students may have little or no prior knowledge. In that case, it is important to engage in activities that clearly present the necessary background.

2. Students then write particular items they already know and particular items they want to know on individual KWL charts. You may further prepare them by eliciting their ideas about what types of information the reading selection should contain. For example, if the class is going to read an article on Cesar Chavez, students should be able to anticipate that there will be information about his family background, his experiences as a migrant farm worker and in union organizing, and some evaluation of his accomplishments. You may also provide additional items to guide students' reading or to emphasize important concepts.

3. After this preparation, students read the selection and jot down information they learn as they read. They look for information that answers their questions or adds to what they know.

4. When the reading is completed, the class discusses what they have learned, what questions have been answered, and what new questions have emerged. You may prompt them about new information that might not have been anticipated.

5. Finally, students organize and synthesize what they have learned—possibly in another graphic organizer—for study or for a possible writing assignment.

Sources

Buehl, D. (2001). *Classroom Strategies for Interactive Learning.* Newark, DE: International Reading Association.

Carr, E.M., and Ogle, D. (1987). "K-W-L Plus: A Strategy for Comprehension and Summarization." *Journal of Reading*, 28:626–631.

Name _____ Class _____ Date _____

KWL Chart

Directions: With your group, brainstorm and list **what you already Know** about in the first column of the following chart. In the second column, write what you **Want to know** or find out from reading the selection. After you read, review your notes and record **what you Learned** in the third column of the chart.

Selection _____

What You Already Know	What You Want to Know	What You Learned

Vocab-o-Gram

Description

Vocab-o-Gram is a productive strategy for both comprehension and vocabulary. It is an appropriate strategy for use with fiction. A Vocab-o-Gram is a classification chart that includes the elements of story structure. Because students in middle grades and high school are familiar with story structure, if they are given some essential words, they can anticipate or predict what might be likely to happen.

Students are given selected words or phrases from a story and asked to organize them according to the story elements. The organized groups of words enable students to formulate ideas and make predictions about the story. After students read, they return to their Vocab-o-Gram charts and reevaluate their predictions and clarify vocabulary as necessary.

Steps

1. Select 10–20 words and phrases from a story that may reflect characters, setting, feelings, key ideas, or events. Present the words to students on the board or on an overhead.

2. Give students a copy of the Vocab-o-Gram chart. Have them work in pairs or small groups to share what they know about the words. They then decide which words give clues to the different elements of a story and place the words in the appropriate category on their charts. They may place words in more than one category.

3. Conduct a class discussion about students' placement of the words and their reasoning for the placement. Have students share their knowledge of words that may be unfamiliar.

4. After students have completed this discussion, they will have formed some preliminary ideas about the story. Have them state their preliminary ideas as predictions about the characters, events, and so on.

5. Suggest that each student also formulate one or two specific questions to answer.

6. After reading, return to the Vocab-o-Gram and refine their ideas. Review the vocabulary and clarify any words by returning to the selection or using reference works.

Source

Blachowicz, C., and Fisher, P.J. (2002). *Teaching Vocabulary in All Classrooms.* Upper Saddle River, NJ: Merrill/Prentice Hall.

Name _____ Class _____ Date _____

Vocab-o-Gram Chart

Directions: Insert the vocabulary in the categories in the first column where you think they might apply. Then, in the second column, make some predictions about the story elements based on the words you placed in the first column.

Selection _____

Words	Predictions
The setting	
The characters	
The problem or goal	
The actions or events	
The resolution	
Other	
What questions do you have?	
Unknown words	

Word Forms

Description

Students benefit from knowing related forms of words. Many of the Vocabulary Builder words with selections have important related forms. A Word Form Chart, similar to the one on the next page, is an excellent way to give students access to related word forms. This chart enables students to readily visualize vocabulary connections and to apply this new terminology in discussion of the selections and in follow-up writing tasks.

Steps

1. Determine which Vocabulary Builder words have other forms that are useful for students to know. Using the blank Word Form Chart provided, insert these new words in the appropriate category: *Noun, Verb, Adjective,* or *Adverb.* Not all words have forms for all parts of speech.

2. Distribute the chart to students and elicit from them any related word forms with which they may already be familiar. Then supply any critical unfamiliar forms. Refrain from supplying related word forms that are beyond the developmental range of your students. For example, when introducing the lesson term *prejudice* (noun) to a group of sixth-grade students with a high percentage of second-language learners and less-proficient readers, it would certainly be beneficial to point out the high-frequency adjective form *prejudiced* but inappropriate and overwhelming to dwell on the verb form *to prejudice,* which occurs mainly in legal contexts.

3. When assigning related word forms for students to identify, clarify the target parts of speech. For example, if you want them to identify only the adjective form of the noun *prejudice,* then place an asterisk in the adjective section on the Word Form Chart. This will prevent students from spinning their wheels trying to identify a part of speech that may not even exist or that may be out of their developmental range or beyond the assigned lesson topic.

4. Have students note that sometimes there are two forms of a particular part of speech. When this occurs, explain—or have students explain—the difference in meaning between the two word forms.

5. Encourage students to refer to their completed Word Form Charts when working on follow-up speaking and writing assignments. Hold them accountable for integrating new words in their speaking and writing and using the appropriate word form by factoring in the application of new vocabulary in your assessment practices, such as rubrics.

Name _____ Class _____ Date _____

Word Form Chart

Selection _____

Noun	Verb	Adjective	Adverb

Response Journals

Description

Response Journals can be set up in a number of ways and used for a variety of purposes. Response Journals are an opportunity for students to interact personally and independently with a piece of literature. Initially, students may be guided in their responses, with a Response Starters sheet, which provides a series of stems to be built into response statements. Later, students may work in a two-column response format, with prepared sheets or in their own notebooks.

Response Journals encourage students to make personal connections with the text, a valuable starting point for constructing their own understanding. As students become accustomed to and proficient with responding in a journal, they can be encouraged or guided to do more text analysis, employing higher-level thinking about the content.

Steps

1. Actively responding in a journal prompts thoughtful reactions to the selection and its relevance to students' lives or to life in general. As they make such connections while reading, students will come to a deeper understanding of the literature. As students are preparing to read a selection or a full-length book on their own, explain to them the reason for and importance of responding to literature. Ask students to give examples of things they might be thinking as they read their favorite genres. Have them be as specific and detailed as they can. Write students' ideas on the board.

2. Explain to students that in addition to the ideas they stated, there are many other things they might think about as they read. Pass out copies of the Response Journal Starters sheet. Review some of the stems on it. Model how you might apply some of them by reading aloud a portion of a selection the class is reading or has recently read. Encourage students to participate.

   If necessary, take time to go through the list of starters with the class to ensure that students have a general understanding of what they mean. You might mention at what points in a selection certain starters may be particularly appropriate.

3. As students are preparing to read a new selection or a full-length book, pass out copies of the Two-Column Response Journal sheet. Model how to use this sheet, applying some of the response starters. Tell students to record their quotations in the left column and their responses to the quotation in the right column, using the response starters. As they use a starter, they may check it off on the sheet. Encourage students to use as many of the starters as they can.

4. When students have finished reading and responding, ask for volunteers to share their quotations and responses or have students share in groups. Encourage disagreement and discussion. Exposure to one another's responses will expand students' views of the responding possibilities. Have students staple the Response Starters sheet to the front of their Two-Column Response sheets. Students may save their work in a folder or notebook. Sharing personal responses is not necessary; it may be valuable as students are learning this strategy, but thereafter the strategy may be better as a personal one.

You may want some students to expand their Two-Column Response Journal sheets into a dialogue journal that they share with a partner. Tell them to add a third column labeled My Partner's Response. Then, have them exchange papers with a partner and react to the partner's responses through comments or questions. Partners should discuss their new ideas and insights at the end of the activity.

5. Point out to students that their responses to any reading are not limited to the response starters. They may respond in other ways as well, depending on their own insights into or feelings about what they are reading. When reading a selection from *Prentice Hall Literature*, they may also respond to the questions in the right margins.

6. Assign or encourage students to use Response Journals when reading any literature on their own. The ongoing practice will heighten their attention to the literary texts they read. Students might like to set up a notebook as a Response Journal and use it exclusively for this purpose.

7. To make students accountable, you might collect and read their Response Journals and provide constructive feedback on them.

Source

Ollmann, H.E. (1992). "Two-Column Response to Literature." *Journal of Reading*, 35:58.

Response Journal Starters

- I wonder what will happen when . . .

- Does this mean that . . . ?

- I notice that . . ., which is interesting because . . .

- There is a lot of truth in this statement because . . .

- Life is like this when . . .

- This reminds me of . . .

- This sounds like another story, . . .

- I think what will happen next is . . .

- If I were this character, I would have . . .

- I bet the next thing this character will do is . . .

- I like the words . . . because . . .

- This description really made me appreciate how . . .

- The author is trying to make us see that . . .

- This is different from my time/culture because . . .

- This seems very realistic/unrealistic because . . .

- I do not like . . . because . . .

- If I were to rewrite this part, I would . . .

- At first I thought . . ., but now I think . . .

- Now I understand that . . .

Name _____ Class _____ Date _____

Two-Column Response Journal

Directions: Use this page for responses as you read. On the left side, copy quotations from the text. Choose sentences or passages that have particular meaning to you, that make you wonder about something, or anything else that strikes you and to which you wish to respond.

In the right column, next to each quotation, write your response. You may interpret the quotation, relate it to your own life, ask questions, evaluate it, comment on the writing style, or make any other kind of response.

Selection _____

Sentence or Passage from Selection	My Thoughts and Comments

Literature Circles

Description

Literature Circles are an excellent way to foster independent reading and responding within a collaborative group environment and an opportunity for students to go beyond their Response Journals. Students in Literature Circles not only collaborate to discover meaning; they develop responsibility and also have the pleasure of reading a good book and discussing it.

A Literature Circle is a temporary group formed to read and discuss books. The circle meets regularly, and each student takes on a specific role in the discussion. These discussions, based on students' own responses, involve a minimum of teacher intervention. Although Literature Circles have a structure and specified roles, they can be modified to accommodate a variety of circumstances and needs.

Steps

1. To introduce Literature Circles, tell students a little about the kinds of reading groups many adults belong to—the group chooses a book, and all the members read and discuss it.

2. To set up your Literature Circles, assign or allow students to choose appropriate titles from the Prentice Hall/Penguin Literature Library. Set up groups of four or five students to read and discuss one book. Interest students in the books by displaying the books in class and telling a little about each one. Allow students to examine the books, by looking at the front and back covers and flipping through the pages.

3. The roles of the participants in Literature Circles are important to the success of this strategy. You may assign roles for the duration of a Literature Circle, or you may have students rotate roles with each meeting. Four roles are essential, but other roles may be accommodated as well. The following roles are essential:
Discussion Director: Creates open-ended questions to guide group discussion.
Literary Luminary: Selects quotations or details from the text to bring to the attention of the group.
Connector: Points out ways that the reading connects to themselves, the group, or the world.
Illustrator: Represents key scenes or ideas from the reading in some kind of drawing.

Literature Circles may also have participants in the following roles:
Summarizer: Prepares a summary of the key points of each reading segment.
Vocabulary Enricher: Clarifies meanings of important or unfamiliar words.

It is important that students become familiar with the roles before they take them on. To help students organize and structure their responses, give each group three or four copies of Roles in Literature Circles. Students may use these sheets as guides and reminders for their roles and to make notes in preparation for the discussion. (They will probably need additional paper to record their ideas for their group discussions.) You might model and practice the roles with a selection the whole class reads together.

Some students may find the defined roles too limiting. Remind them that they are not required to focus only on these roles. Encourage them to think of other roles that group participants might play—for example, someone to get information on various places mentioned in a book.

4. Choose a reasonable time frame for students to finish reading their books. Students then meet once or twice a week, during class, to discuss the book in their Literature Circles. For example, you might allow three weeks for an average-length novel. For the first assignment, have students set up a reading schedule. They must determine the number of pages, with logical starting and stopping points, to read in preparation for each meeting.

5. As students read, encourage them to take notes or use sticky notes to mark passages that contain memorable ideas. They can also make notes using a Two-Column Response Journal.

6. When students meet in their groups, they should run their own discussions. (In the beginning, you will probably need to prompt them with questions or comments if their ideas flounder.) Tell them to refer to *all* the notes they have prepared when they talk about their books, not just the Roles in Literature Circles sheet.

7. When a group has finished a book, you might ask the members to tell the class about it. Encourage them to tell just enough to get other students interested in reading it. When all groups are finished reading, have students make new book choices and form new groups.

Source

Daniels, H. (2002). *Literature Circles: Voice and Choice in Book Clubs and Reading Groups*, 2nd ed. Portland, ME: Stenhouse.

Name _____ Class _____ Date _____

Roles in Literature Circles

Discussion Director: Ask Questions	For example: • How well can I identify with these characters and situations? • What seems likely to happen next? • What events seem likely? unlikely? YOUR IDEAS:
Literary Luminary: Look for the Best Parts	For example: • Identify a section, a piece of dialogue, or an event that really struck you; tell why. • Figure out how to get the group to appreciate this part. YOUR IDEAS:
Connector: Connect Ideas	For example: • Connect to things you have experienced at home, at school, or in your personal life. • Connect to what is going on in the world right now. YOUR IDEAS:
Illustrator: Put Ideas into Pictures	For example: • Draw a picture of an important event or character. • Draw a diagram that shows how you reacted to something in the book. YOUR IDEAS:

Save the Last Word for Me

Description

To become thoughtful, responsive readers, students need to be encouraged to think about more than finding answers to questions or commenting on characters or plot. Save the Last Word for Me is an excellent strategy for developing active and reflective readers by eliciting responses to specific quotations or passages from literature. The small group setting gives students an opportunity to interact meaningfully about a selection or a full-length work as they learn how to respond thoughtfully and completely and to justify their responses. In addition to encouraging those who may be reluctant to speak in front of the full class, the format also gives students time to rehearse their comments by writing them first.

Steps

1. This strategy works well with selections that are rich and potentially interesting to students. Prepare students to read by establishing background knowledge and clarifying vocabulary in your prereading activities. If working with a full-length book, you might apply this strategy to chapters or use it when students have completed the entire work.

2. Have students read the assigned work independently. Instruct them to note three to five statements or ideas that catch their attention as they read. These may be ideas with which they agree or disagree, that they find amusing, surprising, or intriguing, that reveal something about a character or an event in a story, or that are powerfully or eloquently stated. Provide students with sticky notes to mark these ideas.

3. After students have finished reading, give them copies of the Save the Last Word for Me response page. Tell students to go back and copy the statements that caught their attention onto this response sheet in the left column in the boxes above the dotted line. Then, have them paraphrase each statement they quoted—put it in their own words—in the boxes under the dotted line.

   If some students need more instruction or support on paraphrasing, provide a paraphrasing prompt, such as "I think this means _____ because _____."

4. After students have paraphrased each quotation, ask them to react to each. Students can begin by writing one sentence stating their reaction to it. Then students should write two or three sentences explaining or justifying the reaction. Modeling the technique for students at this point is important.

   For students who need more modeling of responding, you could read aloud several paragraphs from the story and note every time an idea strikes you. Model how to respond: agree, disagree, find interesting or surprising, share a personal experience, or relate to something else. Always explain or justify your reaction.

5. After students have written their responses, they gather in groups of three or four. The first student reads one of his or her quotations aloud along with the paraphrase, but not the reaction. The other group members respond to and discuss the quotation. When the other students have responded, the original student then reads his or her reaction, thus having the last word on the quotation. Then, the next person in the group reads his or her quotation and paraphrase, and the procedure continues as before until each person in the group has shared a statement and had the last word on it. You may then continue with another round of statements.

6. When students have finished, bring the class together to debrief. Did writing down ideas make students read more carefully and thoughtfully? Did their group members' responses make them think about their quotations in a different way? What ideas did they hear that were particularly interesting or surprising?

7. As an alternative to the Save the Last Word for Me Response Page, students may use index cards or paper folded in half, one card or sheet per statement.

Sources

Buehl, D. (2001). *Classroom Strategies for Interactive Learning.* Newark, DE: International Reading Association.
Vaughan, J., and Estes, T. (1986). *Reading and Reasoning Beyond the Primary Grades.* Boston: Allyn and Bacon.

Name _____ Class _____ Date _____

Save the Last Word for Me Response Page

My Quotations and Paraphrases	My Reactions

ReQuest (Reciprocal Questioning)

Description

ReQuest, an acronym for Reciprocal Questioning, is an instructional strategy designed by A. V. Manzo to help students develop an active, questioning approach as they read instructional materials. The ReQuest procedure promotes strategic learning by teaching students how to establish appropriate purposes for reading, and it enhances students' comprehension by teaching them to ask their own questions about what they are reading. When students ask themselves questions while reading, they are more likely to comprehend the text and to monitor their comprehension. The approach encourages students to read literature in-depth, noticing significant details and thinking beyond the surface.

It is important that you model effective questioning behaviors during the ReQuest procedure. Less experienced readers need to learn how to move beyond relatively simple text-based questions to more demanding interpretive or applied questions. As students become used to the strategy, they gradually assume more responsibility in the process.

Steps

1. Model the process by reading a brief section of the text aloud. Ask and answer your own questions about the text, progressing from factual recall to questions that stimulate interpretive or applied thinking.

2. After modeling this question-and-response pattern with a brief passage, ask students to read the next section of the text. With less proficient readers, consider reading the section aloud and having them read along silently. Have students take turns asking you questions about what they read, which you will then answer.

3. Ask students to read another segment. Ask them questions, which they answer.

4. Continue to alternate between student-generated questions and teacher-generated questions until the entire designated section has been read.

5. Assign the remaining portion for students to read silently, asking and answering their own questions. Then, lead a wrap-up discussion of the material.

6. Reinforce this questioning technique until students are comfortable applying it on their own. For students who may need more instruction and support, provide a manageable list of potential questions and question types. Many inexperienced younger readers are somewhat familiar with basic questions for narrative texts but need to go beyond the surface.

Sources

Manzo, A.V. (1969). "The ReQuest Procedure." *Journal of Reading*, 13:123–126.
Manzo, A.V., Manzo, U.C., and Estes, T.H. (2001). *Content Area Literacy: Interactive Teaching for Active Learning*, 3rd ed. Hoboken, NJ: John Wiley & Sons.

Question-Answer Relationships (QAR)

Description

Question-Answer Relationships (Raphael, 1982, 1986) is a strategy that helps students differentiate among various types of comprehension questions, enabling them to tackle questions more effectively.

The relationship between questions and the source of answers is not always obvious to students. Some questions are based solely on the text students are reading. These text-based questions may be text explicit ("right there") or text implicit ("think and search").

- **Right there** questions pick up exact words and phrases from the text. Students should be able to find the answers explicitly stated. These types of questions often begin with words like *Who is, Where is, When, What kind of,* and so on.

- **Think and search** questions are more challenging. Information is available in the text but requires integration of the text material. Students have to think about what they have read, search through a selection, and integrate information for an answer. These questions often include words such as *explain, summarize, compare, contrast,* and *what caused.*

Other types of questions require students to use their own knowledge and/or information from the text.

- **Author and you** questions ask students to synthesize what they already know with new information they have just learned. Students will not find ready-made answers in the text. Instead, they will have to put text information together with applicable prior knowledge.

- **On my own** questions test what students know from sources beyond the text. Students can answer these questions without having read the text by drawing on their own knowledge and experience.

Steps

1. Introduce students to the task demands of different types of questions. Explain the types of question-answer relationships and demonstrate them with examples from a selection the class is reading, progressing from factual recall to questions that test students' critical-thinking skills and background knowledge. Explain how and where to find the answers.

2. Once students have grasped the relationships, give them questions labeled by relationship and have them find the answers.

3. As students become competent, pose questions without labels or direct them to the questions in the text and instruct them to develop answers and decide which question-answer relationship applies.

4. Reinforce as necessary when students might be having difficulty answering questions in the text.

Sources

Raphael, T.E. Question-answering Strategies for Children. *The Reading Teacher,* 36:186–190.
Raphael, T.E. "Teaching Question-Answer Relationships Revisited," *The Reading Teacher,* 39:516–522.
Tierney, R.J. and Readence, J.E. (2000). *Reading Strategies and Practices: A Compendium.* Boston: Allyn and Bacon.

Reading Log

Description

A Reading Log with reader's comments and personal responses reflects accumulated reading accomplishments. Reading Logs are often required elements of school portfolios and mandated in state curriculums. Log pages should be kept in the classroom files.

Accurate Reading Logs are diagnostic tools for teachers, providing data of reading patterns and levels. Students can utilize Reading Logs as a tool for comparison, an outline for studying, or a method of activating prior knowledge.

Steps

1. Provide the students with several Reading Log pages. Students translate the number of pages into reading expectations.

2. Explain the type of reading that is to be recorded. It is useful to ask students to record reading in other subject areas as well.

3. Define *comments*. Comments should be a brief reaction to the work with reasons. To differentiate instruction, give a range of questions the students may use to form comments, such as the following scaffolded questions:

   - What did you like or dislike about the main character?
   - What did you learn from the main character?
   - Would you read this book again? Why or why not?
   - If you could talk to the author, what would you suggest be changed in the book? Why?
   - If you were a publisher, would you have published this book? Why or why not?

4. Designate 5 to 10 minutes a week to update Reading Logs. This should be on the same day at approximately the same time so that logging becomes part of the students' routine. Updating logs serves as a reminder to students of their reading accomplishments for the week and can be used as a summary activity.

   Check that the Reading Logs are returned to their designated classroom storage area at the end of each session.

5. Periodically write phrase comments on the Reading Logs so students are aware that you are checking their logs. Comments need not be lengthy or time consuming.

Name _____

Class _____ Date _____

Reading Log

Directions: Use this log to keep a record of the books you read and your comments on those books.

Title	Author	Type of Literature	Date Finished	Comments

Interpretation Chart

Description

This close reading exercise is designed to give students practice in paraphrasing text and integrating the specific idea into the whole work. The Interpretation Chart asks students to choose a quotation that is important thematically, paraphrase the quotation to restate in their own words, and then determine why the quoted line is an important piece of the whole. Charts may be used as a basis for Literature Circle discussions, textual evidence for essays, or in large group discussion.

Steps

1. Choose a chapter or short selection to work with.

2. Preview the reading with students. Ask students to read the selection, noting important passages. Students may underline, use sticky notes, or write down the page number. They should not stop their reading to write down the entire quotation.

3. Ask students to return to the quotations they marked and choose two to copy onto the chart.

4. Model paraphrasing of one quotation. Demonstrate how to change sentence structure and wording.

5. Have students paraphrase one of the quotations.

6. Return to the model and discuss why this quotation is important to the whole work. (You may use a checklist of elements of the novel to help structure students' thinking.)

7. Ask students to write the "Why Is It Important" for their first quotation. Select two or three to read out loud as an informal check on understanding.

8. Students should fill in the chart for the second quotation individually.

9. Check that students are connecting the paraphrased quotation to the third column.

10. Ask students to complete the remainder of the chart.

Name _____ Class _____ Date _____

Interpretation Chart

Directions: Use the following chart to help organize your thoughts on one or more aspects of a work of literature. In the first column, provide quotations from the work. In the second column, paraphrase each of the quotations. Finally, in the third column, discuss why the quoted line is important to the work.

Selection _____

What Does It Say?	What Does It Mean?	Why Is It Important?

Paired Discussion

Description

Paired Discussion encourages students to listen to another point of view and use that information to modify their own thoughts. The use of pairs encourages reluctant speakers to express their opinions. Paired Discussion also reinforces summary and paraphrasing skills and develops interpretation skills.

Preparing the Assignment

Choose a question based on a reading assignment that is appropriate to the middle thinking level of the class. The question should be presented to the students in writing so that they can reread. Write the question on the board, use an overhead, or dictate. Give the students thinking time; the length of time will depend on the depth and breadth of the question you ask.

Rules

- Set a time limit and stick to it.
- Explain that only one person may speak at a time and their partner should not interrupt them. Encourage students to note a question and return to it when their discussion partner is finished speaking.
- Monitor the discussions to see that students are on task.

Steps

1. Check that students have the required text on their desk. Then, give them the question.

2. Allow students 5–10 minutes to think about the question and return to the text to find examples.

3. Have students write their responses in the "My Response" column.

4. One person in the pair reads his or her response. The other person paraphrases the response and writes it down in the "My Partner's Response" column. Repeat this process with the second person in the pair.

5. Allow 5–10 minutes for students to ask each other questions regarding the responses.

6. Break down the third column into two thinking sections for the students. Ask students to individually fill in the "What I Think Now" portion of the third column. Instruct students to reread their statement of "What I Think Now."

7. Ask students to fill in the "and Why" section of the third column and then exchange papers with their partners to read.

8. Summarize the exercise by having volunteers read their sequence. Emphasize that listening to someone else's perspective can modify your own thinking.

Name _____ Class _____ Date _____

Paired Discussion

Directions: When working with a partner in a Paired Discussion, use the following chart to record your responses. In the first column, note your initial responses to the discussion question. Note your partner's responses in the second column. Finally, in the third column, note whether your responses changed as a result of your discussion and explain why or why not.

My Response	My Partner's Response	What I Think Now and Why

Think-Pair-Share

Description

Think-Pair-Share encourages students to verbally respond to open-ended questions and incorporates organizing, applying, and generating thinking and writing skills. This strategy emphasizes thinking time, which forces think-on-their-feet learners to evaluate their ideas and gives students who do not think on their feet adequate time to prepare; hence, it is a valuable tool in differentiated instruction. Think-Pair-Share asks students to consider a teacher-posed question, organize answers, discuss responses with a partner, and develop a response to report to the class. The strategy assures that each student will have verbal discussion practice.

Steps

1. **Preparing the assignment**
   Time: Thinking time should start at three to five minutes depending on the material students have to review. Discussion time should be short, one to three minutes at first, with increased time as students become comfortable with the process.
   Topic: Clarify the topic and define the types of support that are acceptable to validate the topic. Check that the question cannot be answered by a yes or no. Clarify the thinking time stage.
   Roles: Assign partners to create productive matches. Define who is the first speaker. Define behavioral expectations.

2. **Pose a question to the entire class** The question should allow for responses on different thinking levels. Give students two to three minutes to write a paraphrase of the question. Randomly ask students to read their paraphrase as a check on question recognition.

3. **Think** Provide quiet, individual time for students to deal with the question. They may go back to the text, review notes, or organize their thoughts.

4. **Writing to prepare** (Optional) Ask students to write their responses in draft form. This gives the teacher a chance to provide additional clarification, modeling, or examples.

5. **Pair-Share** Remind students of time frames and cue them to begin discussion with their partners. During discussion, the students should take notes on similarities and differences. Listeners should encourage their partner to clarify, explain, and justify responses. Cue students when to switch listener/speaker roles.

6. **Share with the class** After rehearsing and elaborating their responses with a partner, students are invited to share in a whole class discussion.

Source

Kagan, Spencer. (1992). Cooperative Learning. Kagan Cooperative Learning.

Think-Pair-Share

Directions: Use the following chart to help organize your thoughts on your teacher's question. Discuss your answers with your partner.

Paraphrase question: Restate the question in your own words.	
Information gathering: What do I need to gather to answer this question?	
Organizing: How do I put this information together so it forms an answer?	
Writing: What is my answer to the question? How do I support that answer?	
Pair Share: Listener List the points the speaker is making. Underline points that could be clearer.	
Pair Share: Speaker List points that need clarification.	
Response to share with class:	

Give One, Get One

Description

The typical question-and-answer protocols of many classroom discussions require spontaneous processing rather than active listening, conscientious reflection, and articulate responding. Give One, Get One is a productive alternative to the typical teacher-facilitated discussion format. This student-centered strategy allows students to share relevant background knowledge and experiences with partners before reporting new understandings during a unified class discussion. A multimodal strategy builds critical listening, speaking, reading, and writing skills. Students begin with quiet, independent reflection and writing time in response to a focused question or task. They then converse with classmates, one at a time. The goal of each interaction is to explain ideas and to obtain new ideas. After sharing ideas, students add one idea from the partner's list to their own. They then venture on to a new classmate. This procedure continues for a designated time. In the final stage, the teacher facilitates a highly structured, unified class debriefing. One student begins by sharing an idea learned from a peer. The student whose contribution has just been explained is next to report a new idea. Students must actively listen for their idea.

Steps

1. **Pose a thought-provoking question or concrete task** The question may be from any stage of a lesson, to activate prior knowledge, to make predictions and inferences, to assess comprehension, or to apply new understanding. The first few times you work with this strategy, select a question that you are confident all students will be able to answer.

2. **Preparing for participation** Give students five to eight minutes of quiet time to jot down responses. Specify the minimum number of responses you would like to see to push students to think beyond their initial response.

3. **Regrouping** Each student should draw a line after their final idea to differentiate this idea from those to be gathered from classmates. They should then put a check mark next to the two or three ideas he or she perceives as the strongest.

4. **Exchanging ideas** Students are given a set amount of time to share ideas with classmates. After each student finds a partner, the two classmates exchange papers and quietly read each other's ideas. Each student should comment on anything of particular interest on the other's list or ask for clarification. Each student then selects one idea from the other's list and adds it to his or her own list, noting the partner's name next to the idea.

5. **Debriefing** At the end of the Give One, Get One exchange period, the teacher facilitates a unified class debriefing of ideas. Record each idea along with the student's name on the board. This list can later be used as a springboard for practicing or teaching organizational strategies.

Name _____ Class _____ Date _____

Selection _____

Give One, Get One

Directions: Paraphrase the question posed by your teacher. Then, take a few minutes to record your responses to the question. After sharing ideas with class-mates, record one idea from each partner's list on the chart. Make sure to note each partner's name next to his or her idea.

Paraphrase of question:

_____

_____

_____

My ideas:

1. _____

   _____

2. _____

   _____

3. _____

   _____

4. _____

   _____

5. _____

   _____

My Partners' Ideas	My Partners' Names
1.	
2.	
3.	
4.	
5.	

Discussion Guide

As you study literature, you will find that your discussions with other readers will help you develop interpretations of the works you read. Use the following tips to help you practice the good speaking and listening skills necessary for success in group discussions:

- **Communicate effectively** Effective communication requires thinking before speaking. Plan the points that you want to make and decide how you will express them. Organize these points in logical order and cite details from the work to support your ideas. Also, remember to speak clearly, pronouncing words slowly and carefully.

- **Make relevant contributions** Especially when responding to literature, avoid simply summarizing the plot. Instead, consider *what* you think might happen next, *why* events took place as they did, or *how* a writer provoked a response in you. Let your ideas inspire deeper thought or discussion about the literature that you are reading.

- **Consider other ideas and interpretations** One of the exciting parts of literature study is the varied responses that a work can generate in readers. Be open to the idea that many interpretations can be valid. To support your own ideas, point to the events, descriptions, characters, or other literary elements in the work that led to your interpretation. To consider someone else's ideas, decide whether details in the work support the interpretation he or she presents.

- **Ask questions** Get in the habit of asking questions. This can help you clarify your understanding of another reader's ideas. Questions can also be used to call attention to possible areas of confusion or debate or to errors in the speaker's points. When discussions become interactive, you can take your analysis and understanding of a work further.

As you meet with a discussion group, use a chart such as the following to analyze the discussion:

Work Being Discussed:	
Focus Questions:	
Your Response:	Another Student's Response:
Supporting Evidence:	Supporting Evidence:
One New Idea That You Considered About the Work During the Discussion:	

Writing Rubrics
Listening and Speaking Rubrics

Rubrics for Self-Assessment
Autobiographical Narrative

Evaluate your autobiographical narrative using one of the following rubrics:

Autobiographical Narrative—4-point rubric

	Audience and Purpose	Organization	Elaboration	Use of Language
Score 4	Contains details that engage the audience	Presents events that create an interesting narrative; told from a consistent point of view	Contains details that create vivid characters; contains dialogue that develops characters and plot	Uses language to create a tone; contains no errors in grammar, punctuation, or spelling
Score 3	Contains details appropriate for an audience	Presents a sequence of events; told from a specific point of view	Contains details that develop characters and describe setting; uses dialogue	Uses vivid words; contains few errors in grammar, punctuation, and spelling
Score 2	Contains few details that appeal to an audience	Presents a confusing sequence of events; contains a point of view that is inconsistent	Contains characters and setting; contains some dialogue	Uses clichés and trite expressions; contains some errors in grammar, punctuation, and spelling
Score 1	Is not written for a specific audience	Presents no logical order; is told from no consistent point of view	Contains few or no details to develop characters or setting; no dialogue is provided	Uses uninspired words; has many errors in grammar, punctuation, and spelling

Autobiographical Narrative—5-point rubric

Criteria	Rating Scale				
	Not Very				Very
Focus: How clearly do you establish yourself as the main character?	1	2	3	4	5
Organization: How effectively do you organize the sequence of events?	1	2	3	4	5
Support/Elaboration: How well do you use details to describe scenes and incidents?	1	2	3	4	5
Style: How well do you use strong verbs and adjectives to establish your characters and setting?	1	2	3	4	5
Conventions: How correct is your grammar, especially your use of punctuation?	1	2	3	4	5

Autobiographical Narrative—6-point rubric

	Audience and Purpose	Organization	Elaboration	Use of Language
Score 6	Provides a clear insight about an experience; contains details that engage the audience	Organizes events to relate an engaging and clear narrative; told from a consistent point of view	Contains rich details that shape vivid characters; uses dialogue that develops characters and plot	Uses an excellent variety of sentence beginnings and good word choices; contains no errors in spelling, grammar, or punctuation
Score 5	Addresses a clear reason for writing; contains details that appeal to an audience	Presents a clear sequence of events; told from a specific point of view	Contains details that develop characters and describe setting; uses dialogue that develops characters	Uses a good variety of sentence beginnings and word choices; contains few errors in spelling, grammar, or punctuation
Score 4	Includes some details that contribute to its purpose and that appeal to an audience	Is consistently organized, although perhaps simplistically	Develops characters with details but some vague words; uses dialogue	Sentence structures and word choices are appropriate; errors in spelling, grammar, or punctuation may occur, but they do not interfere with reader understanding
Score 3	Contains few details that contribute to its purpose or appeal to an audience	May have organization in some parts but lacks organization in other parts	Provides some details to develop characters; uses some dialogue	Introduces some variety in sentence beginnings and word choices; errors in spelling, grammar, or punctuation occasionally interfere with reader understanding
Score 2	Minimal attempt to address a specific audience or purpose for writing	Presents a confusing sequence of events	Limited details in support of the story; contains little or no dialogue	Problematic sentence structures and frequent inaccuracies in word choices; errors in spelling, grammar, and punctuation hinder reader understanding
Score 1	Is not written for a specific audience or purpose	Presents no logical order of events; may be too brief to assess organization	Contains few or no details to develop characters or setting; does not use dialogue	Uses a monotonous pattern of sentence beginnings and incorrect word choices; many errors in spelling, grammar, and punctuation

Rubrics for Self-Assessment
Persuasive Essay

Evaluate your persuasive essay using one of the following rubrics:

Persuasive Essay—4-point rubric

	Audience and Purpose	Organization	Elaboration	Use of Language
Score 4	Presents a clear opinion that is strongly supported by convincing and persuasive techniques suited to the audience	Structures ideas and arguments in a sustained, persuasive, and sophisticated way	Supports ideas and arguments with precise, convincing, and relevant examples; provides many specific and well-elaborated reasons	Does not include any empty or hedging words; introduces few, if any, mechanical and grammatical errors
Score 3	Presents an opinion that is supported by somewhat convincing and persuasive techniques suited to the audience	Structures ideas and arguments in a sustained and persuasive way	Supports ideas and arguments with convincing and relevant examples; provides some specific reasons	Includes a few empty or hedging words; introduces a few mechanical and grammatical errors
Score 2	Presents a somewhat vague opinion with weak persuasive techniques that are not well suited to the audience	Structures ideas and arguments in a somewhat persuasive way	Supports ideas and arguments with some relevant examples; provides one or two specific reasons	Includes a noticeable number of empty or hedging words; introduces some mechanical and grammatical errors
Score 1	Presents a vague opinion that is not supported by persuasive techniques	Fails to structure ideas and arguments in a persuasive way	Does not support ideas and arguments with reasonable or relevant examples; provides no specific reasons	Includes many empty or hedging words; introduces many mechanical and grammatical errors

Persuasive Essay—5-point rubric

Criteria	Rating Scale				
	Not Very				Very
Focus: How clear is your thesis statement?	1	2	3	4	5
Organization: How effectively do you organize your arguments?	1	2	3	4	5
Support/Elaboration: How well do you use evidence, including facts and examples, to support your position?	1	2	3	4	5
Style: How well do you use convincing language?	1	2	3	4	5
Conventions: How correct is your grammar, especially your use of commonly confused words?	1	2	3	4	5

Persuasive Essay—6-point rubric

	Audience and Purpose	Organization	Elaboration	Use of Language
Score 6	Clearly states the author's position and effectively persuades the reader of the validity of the author's argument	Well organized, with strong transitions helping to link words and ideas	Develops its arguments with specific, well-elaborated support	Varies sentence structures and makes good word choices; very few errors in spelling, grammar, or punctuation
Score 5	Clearly states the author's position, and persuades the reader	Clearly organized, although an occasional lapse may occur	Develops its arguments with specific support	Some sentence variety and good word choices; some errors in spelling, grammar, or punctuation, but they do not interfere with reader understanding
Score 4	States a position and adequately attempts to persuade the reader	Is consistently organized, although perhaps simplistically	Provides some elaborated support of the author's position	Sentence structures and word choices are appropriate; errors in spelling, grammar, or punctuation may occur but they do not interfere with reader understanding
Score 3	Although a position may be stated, either it is unclear or undeveloped	May have organization in some parts but lacks organization in other parts	The support of the position may be brief, repetitive, or irrelevant	Inconsistent control of sentence structures and incorrect word choices; errors in spelling, grammar, or punctuation occasionally interfere with reader understanding
Score 2	Either a position is not clearly given or little attempt is made at persuasion	Very disorganized and not easy to follow	The support of the position is not well developed	Problematic sentence structures and frequent inaccuracies in word choices; errors in spelling, grammar, and punctuation hinder reader understanding
Score 1	Little effort is made to persuade because there is no position taken or because no support is given	Lacks organization and is confusing and difficult to follow; may be too brief to assess organization	Lacks support	Little or no control over sentences and incorrect word choices may cause confusion; many errors in spelling, grammar, and punctuation severely hinder reader understanding

Rubrics for Self-Assessment
Reflective Essay

Evaluate your reflective essay using one of the following rubrics:

Reflective Essay—4-point rubric

	Audience and Purpose	Organization	Elaboration	Use of Language
Score 4	Clearly explores the significance of a personal experience or condition; effectively presents an insight about life	Narrates a sequence of events that clearly forms the basis of an insight; maintains a balance in describing specific incidents and relating them to more general and abstract ideas	Effectively uses rhetorical strategies; draws clear comparisons between specific incidents and broader themes	Uses language to consistently enhance subtlety of meaning and tone; introduces few, if any, errors
Score 3	Explores the significance of a personal experience or condition; clearly presents an insight about life	Narrates a sequence of events that clearly conveys an insight; describes specific incidents and relates them to more general and abstract ideas	Uses rhetorical strategies; draws comparisons between specific incidents and broader themes	Uses language to convey some subtlety of meaning and tone; introduces few, if any, errors
Score 2	Addresses the significance of a personal experience or condition; alludes to an insight about life	Narrates a sequence of events that vaguely relates to an insight; attempts to connect the essay's insight to the specific incidents described	Somewhat uses rhetorical strategies; draws a few comparisons between specific incidents and broader themes	Uses language to convey basic meanings; includes some mechanical and grammatical errors
Score 1	Vaguely describes a personal experience; fails to present an insight about life	Includes some events that indicate a sense of an insight; makes one or two associations among the specific incidents described	Uses rhetorical strategies ineffectively or not at all; vaguely compares specific incidents to a broader theme	Does not present clear meanings; includes many mechanical and grammatical errors

Reflective Essay—5-point rubric

Criteria	Rating Scale				
	Not Very				Very
Focus: How clearly do you state your general view?	1	2	3	4	5
Organization: How logical is your organization?	1	2	3	4	5
Support/Elaboration: How well do you describe the incidents that support your beliefs?	1	2	3	4	5
Style: How well do you establish a personal tone?	1	2	3	4	5
Conventions: How correct is your grammar, especially your use of commas?	1	2	3	4	5

Reflective Essay—6-point rubric

	Audience and Purpose	Organization	Elaboration	Use of Language
Score 6	Clearly explores the significance of a personal experience or condition; effectively presents an insight about life	Conveys a sequence of events that clearly forms the basis of an insight; maintains balance in describing specific incidents and relating them to more general and abstract ideas	Effectively uses rhetorical strategies; draws clear comparisons between specific incidents and broader themes	Consistently enhances subtlety of meaning and tone; introduces few, if any, mechanical or grammar errors
Score 5	Explores the significance of a personal experience or condition; clearly presents an insight about life	Conveys a sequence of events that clearly relates to an insight; describes specific incidents and relates them to more general and abstract ideas	Uses rhetorical strategies; draws comparisons between specific incidents and broader themes	Enhances subtlety of meaning and tone; introduces a few mechanical and grammar errors
Score 4	Addresses the significance of a personal experience or condition; presents an insight about life	Conveys a sequence of events that relates to an insight; shapes the essay somewhat around the incidents of the experience described	Uses rhetorical strategies; draws several comparisons between specific incidents and broader themes	Presents meaning and tone; introduces some mechanical and grammar errors
Score 3	Attempts to describe a personal experience; alludes to an insight about life	Conveys a sequence of events that vaguely relates to an insight; makes several associations among the incidents of the experience described	Somewhat uses rhetorical strategies; draws a few comparisons between specific incidents and broader themes	Covers basic meanings; introduces mechanical and grammar errors that occasionally interfere with reader understanding
Score 2	Vaguely describes a personal experience; leaves insight about life unclear	Includes some events that indicate a sense of insight; makes one or two associations among the incidents described	Uses rhetorical strategies ineffectively; draws a vague comparison between specific incidents and a broader theme	Presents vague meanings; contains mechanical and grammar errors that hinder reader understanding
Score 1	Little or no attempt to describe a personal experience; fails to present an insight about life	Presents no logical order of events; fails to make associations among the incidents of the experience described	Fails to use rhetorical strategies; does not draw comparisons between incidents and theme	Does not present clear meanings; contains many errors in spelling, grammar, and punctuation that severely hinder reader understanding

Rubrics for Self-Assessment
Job Portfolio

Evaluate your job portfolio using one of the following rubrics:

Job Portfolio—4-point rubric

	Audience and Purpose	Organization	Elaboration	Use of Language
Score 4	Effectively provides a summary of education, achievements, work experience, and relevant skills; presented in chronological order	Successfully presents information with a consistent organization	Includes the most essential details; clearly explains their significance and relevance to the position being sought	Strong action words are used to describe all skills; contains no errors in spelling and grammar
Score 3	Provides a general summary of education, achievements, work experience, and some skills; presented in chronological order	Presents information with organization in most parts	Includes mostly essential details; somewhat explains their significance and relevance to the position being sought	Action words are used to describe most skills; contains few errors in spelling and grammar
Score 2	Provides an incomplete summary of education, achievements, work experience, and limited relevant skills	Shows inconsistency in overall organization	Includes random details that may or may not be significant to the position being sought	Action words are used to describe some skills; contains some errors in spelling and grammar
Score 1	Does not provide a summary of education, achievements, and work experience; lacks a logical order	Demonstrates a lack of organizational strategy	Fails to include significant details; fails to explain their relevance to the position being sought	No action words are used to describe skills; contains many errors in spelling and grammar

Job Portfolio—5-point rubric

Criteria	Rating Scale				
	Not Very				Very
Focus: How well does the résumé convey job and life experiences?	1	2	3	4	5
Organization: How well do you employ an easy-to-understand format?	1	2	3	4	5
Support/Elaboration: How appropriate are the specific details of the résumé for the type of work sought?	1	2	3	4	5
Style: How direct and active is your use of language?	1	2	3	4	5
Conventions: How correct is your spelling and your formatting?	1	2	3	4	5

Job Portfolio—6-point rubric

	Audience and Purpose	Organization	Elaboration	Use of Language
Score 6	Effectively provides a summary of education, achievements, work experience, and relevant skills; presented in chronological order	Successfully presents information with a consistent organization	Includes the most essential details; clearly explains their significance and relevance to the position being sought	Strong action words are used to describe all skills; contains no errors in spelling and grammar
Score 5	Provides a clear summary of education, achievements, work experience, and skills; presented in chronological order	Presents information with a consistent organization	Includes essential details; explains their significance and relevance to the position being sought	Action words are used to describe most skills; contains few errors in spelling and grammar
Score 4	Provides a general summary of education, achievements, work experience, and some skills; presented in chronological order	Presents information with organization in most parts	Includes mostly essential details; somewhat explains their significance and relevance to the position being sought	Action words are used to describe some skills; contains some errors in spelling and grammar
Score 3	Provides a partial summary of education, achievements, work experience, and few relevant skills	May have organization in some parts but lacks organization in other parts	Includes some essential details; explains little of their significance and relevance to the position being sought	Some action words are used to describe a few skills; contains some errors in spelling and grammar
Score 2	Provides an incomplete summary of education, achievements, work experience, and limited relevant skills	Shows inconsistency in overall organization	Includes random details that may or may not be significant to the position being sought	Few action words are used to describe skills; contains many errors in spelling and grammar
Score 1	Does not provide a summary of education, achievements, and work experience; lacks a logical order	Demonstrates a lack of organizational strategy	Fails to include significant details; fails to explain their relevance to the position being sought	No action words are used to describe skills; contains numerous errors in spelling and grammar

Rubrics for Self-Assessment
Research Paper

Evaluate your research paper using one of the following rubrics:

Research Paper—4-point rubric

	Audience and Purpose	Organization	Elaboration	Use of Language
Score 4	Focuses on a clearly stated thesis, starting from a well-framed question; gives complete citations	Presents information in a logical order; emphasizes details of central importance	Draws clear conclusions from information gathered from multiple sources	Shows overall clarity and fluency; contains few mechanical errors
Score 3	Focuses on a clearly stated thesis; gives citations	Presents information in a logical order	Draws conclusions from information gathered from multiple sources	Shows good sentence variety; contains some errors in spelling, punctuation, or usage
Score 2	Focuses mainly on the chosen topic; gives some citations	Presents information logically, but organization is poor in places	Explains and interprets some information	Uses awkward or overly simple sentences; contains many mechanical errors
Score 1	Presents information without a clear focus; few or no citations	Presents information in a scattered and disorganized manner	Presents information with little or no interpretation or synthesis	Contains incomplete thoughts and many mechanical errors

Research Paper—5-point rubric

Criteria	Rating Scale				
	Not Very				Very
Focus: How clear and accurate is your thesis statement?	1	2	3	4	5
Organization: How logical and well documented is your presentation?	1	2	3	4	5
Support/Elaboration: How well do you analyze and compare source materials?	1	2	3	4	5
Style: How clearly and effectively do you state your conclusions?	1	2	3	4	5
Conventions: According to an accepted format, how complete and accurate are your citations?	1	2	3	4	5

Research Paper—6-point rubric

	Audience and Purpose	Organization	Elaboration	Use of Language
Score 6	Focuses on a clearly stated thesis, starting from a well-framed question	Well organized, with strong transitions helping to link words and ideas	Provides information, facts, and details in support of thesis; emphasizes details of greatest importance	Varies sentence structures and makes good word choices; very few errors in spelling, grammar, or punctuation
Score 5	Focuses on a clearly stated thesis; gives citations	Clearly organized, although an occasional lapse may occur	Provides information, facts, and details in support of thesis; some emphasis on more important details	Some sentence variety and good word choices; some errors in spelling, grammar, or punctuation, but they do not interfere with reader understanding
Score 4	Focuses on thesis	Is consistently organized, although perhaps simplistically	Provides information, facts, and details in support of thesis	Sentence structures and word choices are appropriate; errors in spelling, grammar, or punctuation may occur, but they do not interfere with reader understanding
Score 3	Thesis may be clear, but focus does not remain consistently on it	May have organization in some parts but lacks organization in other parts	Some information, facts, and details about thesis but with extraneous, ill-chosen, or unnecessary details	Inconsistent control of sentence structures, and incorrect word choices; errors in spelling, grammar, or punctuation occasionally interfere with reader understanding
Score 2	Little emphasis on a single, clear thesis	Very disorganized and not easy to follow	Information or details in support of thesis are undeveloped or unclear	Problematic sentence structures and frequent inaccuracies in word choices; errors in spelling, grammar, and punctuation hinder reader understanding
Score 1	No focus on a single, clear thesis	Lacks organization and is confusing and difficult to follow; may be too brief to assess organization	No clear support of a thesis in the form of information, facts, or details	Little or no control over sentences and incorrect word choices may cause confusion; many errors in spelling, grammar, and punctuation severely hinder reader understanding

Rubrics for Self-Assessment
Multimedia Report

Evaluate your multimedia report using one of the following rubrics:

Multimedia Report—4-point rubric

	Audience and Purpose	Organization	Elaboration	Use of Language
Score 4	Generates a clear and creative presentation; uses the audience's responses to revise the script accordingly	Structures ideas in a sustained and sophisticated way; uses and edits media aptly and monitors for quality	Combines text, images, and sound skillfully; uses precise and relevant media examples to enhance ideas	Uses language in natural, fresh, and vivid ways to establish a specific tone; follows a distinct script format
Score 3	Generates a clear and complete presentation; uses the audience's responses to revise the script	Structures ideas consistently; uses and edits media aptly and monitors for quality	Combines text, images, and sound skillfully; uses media to support ideas with relevant examples	Uses language in natural ways to establish a specific tone; follows an appropriate script format
Score 2	Generates a complete presentation; notes the audience's responses and revises somewhat accordingly	Structures ideas somewhat consistently; uses media, but quality is inconsistent	Combines text, images, and sound; uses media to support ideas with some examples	Uses language in somewhat natural ways, but an inconsistent tone is achieved; follows a vague script format
Score 1	Generates an incomplete presentation; fails to note the audience's responses	Structure ideas inconsistently; uses media inappropriately, and quality is inconsistent	Uses text, images, and sound, but they are not combined or used effectively	Uses language in ineffective ways, and an inconsistent tone is achieved; script format is unrecognizable

Multimedia Report—5-point rubric

Criteria	Rating Scale				
	Not Very				Very
Focus: How clearly do you present your topic?	1	2	3	4	5
Organization: How well do you organize the presentation of information?	1	2	3	4	5
Support/Elaboration: How well do you integrate video and audio elements to support each aspect of your topic?	1	2	3	4	5
Style: How coherent and well paced is the flow of sound, images, and information?	1	2	3	4	5
Conventions: How correct is the grammar, spelling, and punctuation in your presentation materials?	1	2	3	4	5

Multimedia Report—6-point rubric

	Audience and Purpose	Organization	Elaboration	Use of Language
Score 6	Generates a clear and creative presentation; uses the audience's responses to revise the script accordingly	Structures ideas in a sustained and sophisticated way; uses and edits media aptly and monitors for quality	Combines text, images, and sound skillfully; uses precise and relevant media examples to enhance ideas	Uses language in natural, fresh, and vivid ways to establish a specific tone; varies sentences for interest
Score 5	Generates a clear and complete presentation; uses the audience's responses to revise the script	Structures ideas consistently; uses and edits media aptly and monitors for quality	Combines text, images, and sound skillfully; uses media to support ideas with relevant examples	Uses language in natural ways to establish a specific tone; varies sentences for interest
Score 4	Generates a complete presentation; notes the audience's responses and revises somewhat accordingly	Structures ideas appropriately; uses mostly appropriate media to organize and present information	Combines text, images, and sound; uses media to support ideas with some examples	Uses language to establish a somewhat specific tone; demonstrates adequate sentence variety
Score 3	Generates a presentation; makes minor revisions to script based on the audience's responses	Structures ideas somewhat consistently; uses media, but quality is inconsistent	Uses text, images, and sound; occasionally uses media to support some ideas	Uses language in somewhat natural ways, but an inconsistent tone is achieved; varies sentences somewhat
Score 2	Generates a somewhat incomplete presentation; minimal attempt is made to revise script	Structures ideas inconsistently; uses media inappropriately, and quality is inconsistent	Uses components that are not combined or used effectively	Uses language in ineffective ways, and an inconsistent tone is achieved; sentences are static, and their structure is repetitive
Score 1	Presents an incomplete presentation; fails to note the audience's responses	Fails to use appropriate media to organize and present information	Uses components with little or no relation to the material	Uses strained language; tone is unclear; little or no control over sentences

Rubrics for Self-Assessment
Cause-and-Effect Essay

Evaluate your cause-and-effect essay using one of the following rubrics:

Cause-and-Effect Essay—4-point rubric

	Audience and Purpose	Organization	Elaboration	Use of Language
Score 4	Consistently targets an audience; clearly identifies purpose in thesis statement	Presents a clear and consistent organizational strategy to show cause and effect	Successfully links causes with effects; fully elaborates connections among ideas	Uses words precisely; presents very few mechanical errors
Score 3	Targets an audience; identifies purpose in thesis statement	Presents a clear organizational strategy with occasional inconsistencies; shows cause and effect	Links causes with effects; elaborates connections among most ideas	Uses words precisely; presents few mechanical errors
Score 2	Misses a target audience by including a wide range of word choices and details; presents no clear purpose	Presents an inconsistent organizational strategy; creates an illogical presentation of causes and effects	Links some causes with some effects; elaborates connections among most ideas	Contains some imprecise words; presents many mechanical errors
Score 1	Addresses no specific audience or purpose	Demonstrates a lack of organizational strategy; creates a confusing presentation	Develops and elaborates no links between causes and effects	Demonstrates poor use of words; presents many mechanical errors

Cause-and-Effect Essay—5-point rubric

Criteria	Rating Scale				
	Not Very				Very
Focus: How clearly do you identify the cause-and-effect relationship you explore?	1	2	3	4	5
Organization: How consistently and appropriately are ideas organized?	1	2	3	4	5
Support/Elaboration: How successfully are causes and effects linked?	1	2	3	4	5
Style: How clearly do transitions convey ideas?	1	2	3	4	5
Conventions: How correct is your grammar, especially your use of pronouns?	1	2	3	4	5

Cause-and-Effect Essay—6-point rubric

	Audience and Purpose	Organization	Elaboration	Use of Language
Score 6	Clearly identifies a cause-and-effect situation and effectively targets audience	Well organized, with strong transitions helping to link words and ideas	Effectively links causes with effects through relevant and elaborated support and details	Varies sentence structures and makes good word choices; very few errors in spelling, grammar, or punctuation
Score 5	Clearly identifies a cause-and-effect situation and targets audiences	Clearly organized, although an occasional lapse may occur	Links causes with effects through relevant support and details	Some sentence variety and good word choices; some errors in spelling, grammar, or punctuation, but they do not interfere with reader understanding
Score 4	Identifies a cause-and-effect situation and adequately addresses audience	Is consistently organized, although perhaps simplistically	Links causes with effects with some support	Sentence structures and word choices are appropriate; errors in spelling, grammar, or punctuation may occur, but they do not interfere with reader understanding
Score 3	A cause-and-effect situation may be identified, but it is not clear; target audience may not be addressed	May have organization in some parts but lacks organization in other parts	Although some support linking cause and effect may be present, it is not fully or consistently developed	Inconsistent control of sentence structures, and incorrect word choices; errors in spelling, grammar, or punctuation occasionally interfere with reader understanding
Score 2	Only a minimal attempt at linking a cause and effect; either topic is unclear or support is limited	Very disorganized and not easy to follow	Support is very unclear or very undeveloped	Problematic sentence structures and frequent inaccuracies in word choices; errors in spelling, grammar, and punctuation hinder reader understanding
Score 1	Not fully engaged in the task; a cause and effect may not be identified	Lacks organization and is confusing and difficult to follow; may be too brief to assess organization	Lacks supports or no attempt is made to support the connection between cause and effect	Little or no control over sentences and incorrect word choices may cause confusion; many errors in spelling, grammar, and punctuation severely hinder reader understanding

Rubrics for Self-Assessment
Short Story

Evaluate your short story using one of the following rubrics:

Short Story—4-point rubric

	Audience and Purpose	Organization	Elaboration	Use of Language
Score 4	Contains details that create a tone to engage the audience	Presents events that create an interesting and clear narrative; told from a consistent point of view	Contains details that provide insight into characters; contains dialogue that reveals characters and furthers the plot	Uses word choices and tone to reveal story's theme; contains no errors in grammar, punctuation, or spelling
Score 3	Contains details and language that appeal to an audience	Presents a sequence of events; told from a specific point of view	Contains details and dialogue that develop characters	Uses interesting and fresh word choices; contains few errors in grammar, punctuation, and spelling
Score 2	Contains few details that contribute to its purpose or appeal to an audience	Presents a confusing sequence of events; contains inconsistent points of view	Contains characters and setting; contains some dialogue	Uses clichés and trite expressions; contains some errors in grammar, punctuation, and spelling
Score 1	Contains no purpose; is not written for a specific audience	Presents no logical order; is told from no consistent point of view	Contains few or no details to develop characters or setting; no dialogue is provided	Uses uninspired word choices; has many errors in grammar, punctuation, and spelling

Short Story—5-point rubric

Criteria	Rating Scale				
	Not Very				Very
Focus: How effectively does the story convey a theme?	1	2	3	4	5
Organization: How well does the plot build to a climax?	1	2	3	4	5
Support/Elaboration: How effectively have descriptions been brought to life with rich sensory details?	1	2	3	4	5
Style: How effectively does the story show a change or growth in the main character?	1	2	3	4	5
Conventions: How correct is your use of spelling, grammar, and punctuation?	1	2	3	4	5

Short Story—6-point rubric

	Audience and Purpose	Organization	Elaboration	Use of Language
Score 6	Presents an unusual perspective on a conflict; captures the imagination and interest of the audience	Presents a clear sequence of events in a logical order; told from a consistent point of view	Provides rich details and/or illuminating illustrations; incorporates apt, striking word choices; contains dialogue that develops characters and furthers the plot	Demonstrates overall clarity and fluency; presents very few errors in grammar, punctuation, or spelling
Score 5	Presents a series of events leading to a clear conflict; contains details that appeal to an audience	Displays a clear sequence of events; told from a specific point of view	Contains many details that develop characters and plot; makes effective use of dialogue	Demonstrates good sentence variety and word choices; presents few errors in grammar, punctuation, and/or spelling
Score 4	Includes several details that contribute to its purpose or that appeal to an audience	Presents a sequence of events with some inconsistencies of organization	Provides details but some vague words; includes good use of dialogue	Demonstrates adequate sentence variety and word choices; contains some errors in grammar, punctuation, and spelling
Score 3	Contains few details that contribute to its purpose or that appeal to an audience	Presents a somewhat confusing sequence of events; contains inconsistent points of view	Provides some details through limited word choices; includes some use of dialogue	Uses clichés and trite expressions; contains several errors in grammar, punctuation, and spelling
Score 2	Presents little conflict or narrative; some ideas conflict with the narration of the story	Presents a weak or unclear connection between ideas or events	Contains limited amount of details; includes inadequate dialogue	Uses awkward or overly simple sentence structures; presents numerous errors in grammar, punctuation, and spelling
Score 1	Contains no conflict or narrative; is not written for a specific audience	Presents no logical order; lacks a consistent point of view	Contains few or no details to develop characters; does not provide dialogue	Includes incomplete thoughts; creates confusion through errors in grammar, punctuation, and spelling

Rubrics for Self-Assessment
Problem-and-Solution Essay

Evaluate your problem-and-solution essay using one of the following rubrics:

Problem-and-Solution Essay—4-point rubric

	Audience and Purpose	Organization	Elaboration	Use of Language
Score 4	Contains language and details to engage audience and accomplish the purpose	Is organized consistently, logically, and effectively	Has a solution that is clearly laid out, along with details that support or explain it	Contains precise words and no redundancies; contains no errors in grammar, punctuation, or spelling
Score 3	Contains language and details appropriate for audience and that help contribute to overall effect	Has a consistent organization	Has a solution that is supported with details	Contains effective words and few redundancies; contains few errors in grammar, punctuation, and spelling
Score 2	Contains some language and details not suited for audience; contains some details that detract from the purpose	Has an inconsistent organization	Has a stated solution but contains few details to support it	Contains few precise words and some redundancies; contains some errors in grammar, punctuation, and spelling
Score 1	Contains language and details that are not geared for a particular audience; has an unclear purpose	Is disorganized and confusing	Has an unclear solution, and no details are given to support it	Contains imprecise words and many redundancies; contains many errors in grammar, punctuation, and spelling

Problem-and-Solution Essay—5-point rubric

Criteria	Not Very	Rating Scale			Very
Focus: How clearly do you state a significant problem?	1	2	3	4	5
Organization: How well organized is your description of the problem and its solution?	1	2	3	4	5
Support/Elaboration: How well do you provide details and examples to describe and evaluate the problem?	1	2	3	4	5
Style: How well do you use a variety of sentences to express your solution?	1	2	3	4	5
Conventions: How correct is your usage, especially your use of appropriate word meanings?	1	2	3	4	5

Problem-and-Solution Essay—6-point rubric

	Audience and Purpose	Organization	Elaboration	Use of Language
Score 6	Clearly identifies problem and proposes solution; addresses target audience with ability to implement change	Well organized, with strong transitions helping to link words and ideas	Provides relevant details and statistics to effectively support solution	Varies sentence structures and makes good word choices; very few errors in spelling, grammar, or punctuation
Score 5	Clearly identifies problem and proposes solution; addresses target audience	Clearly organized, although an occasional lapse may occur	Provides a solution supported with some details	Some sentence variety and good word choices; some errors in spelling, grammar, or punctuation, but they do not interfere with reader understanding
Score 4	Identifies problem and proposes solution; generally addresses target audience	Is consistently organized, although perhaps simplistically	Provides some support for solution	Sentence structures and word choices are appropriate; errors in spelling, grammar, or punctuation may occur, but they do not interfere with reader understanding
Score 3	Although a problem and solution may be identified, they are not fully linked or support may be undeveloped	May have organization in some parts but lacks organization in other parts	Support for solution may be undeveloped or unspecific	Inconsistent control of sentence structures, and incorrect word choices; errors in spelling, grammar, or punctuation occasionally interfere with reader understanding
Score 2	Some attempt may be made to identify a problem and solution, but either the topic is unclear or the support is limited	Very disorganized and not easy to follow	Limited support for ideas; vague, undeveloped ideas	Problematic sentence structures and frequent inaccuracies in word choices; errors in spelling, grammar, and punctuation hinder reader understanding
Score 1	Little or no attempt is made to address the prompt; response is unfocused or undeveloped	Lacks organization and is confusing and difficult to follow; may be too brief to assess organization	Lacks support; no details or specifics	Little or no control over sentences and incorrect word choices may cause confusion; many errors in spelling, grammar, and punctuation severely hinder reader understanding

Rubrics for Self-Assessment
Business Letter

Evaluate your business letter using one of the following rubrics:

Business Letter—4-point rubric

	Audience and Purpose	Organization	Elaboration	Use of Language
Score 4	Formally and clearly provides purposeful information; addresses the intended audience appropriately	Follows a conventional style for business documents; uses a uniform font and spacing; effectively organizes information	Clearly states and supports the reasons for writing; provides pertinent and appropriate information	Uses widely varied levels, patterns, and types of language to achieve intended effects and aid comprehension; introduces few, if any, mechanical errors
Score 3	Formally provides purposeful information; addresses the intended audience appropriately	Follows a conventional style for business documents; uses a uniform font and spacing; logically organizes information	States and supports the reasons for writing; provides appropriate information	Uses varied levels, patterns, and types of language to achieve intended effects and aid comprehension; introduces a few mechanical errors
Score 2	Formally provides information; does not clearly address the intended audience	Follows some formatting for business writing; logically organizes most information	States a reason for writing but needs more support for it; provides mostly appropriate information	Uses some variety in levels, patterns, and types of language; introduces some mechanical errors
Score 1	Uses informal language; does not address the intended audience appropriately	Uses an inappropriate format for business writing; inconsistently or randomly presents information	Fails to state the reasons for writing; does not provide enough appropriate information	Uses little variety in levels, patterns, and types of language; introduces many mechanical errors

Business Letter—5-point rubric

Criteria	Rating Scale				
	Not Very				Very
Focus: How clearly do you state your purpose?	1	2	3	4	5
Organization: How well does the letter incorporate a heading, an inside address, a greeting, the body, a closing, and a signature?	1	2	3	4	5
Support/Elaboration: How effectively do you provide background information?	1	2	3	4	5
Style: How well does the letter use clear, formal language to communicate courteously?	1	2	3	4	5
Conventions: How effectively does the letter follow conventional formats, fonts, style, and spacing?	1	2	3	4	5

Business Letter—6-point rubric

	Audience and Purpose	Organization	Elaboration	Use of Language
Score 6	Formally and clearly provides purposeful information; consistently addresses the intended audience appropriately	Follows a conventional style for formal business letters; uses a uniform font and spacing; effectively and logically organizes information	Clearly states and supports the reasons for writing; highlights central ideas or images	Uses formal language that communicates briefly, clearly, and courteously; introduces few, if any, grammatical or mechanical errors
Score 5	Formally provides purposeful information; addresses the intended audience appropriately	Follows a conventional style for formal business letters; uses a uniform font and spacing; logically organizes information	States and supports the reasons for writing; lists central ideas or images	Uses formal language that communicates clearly and courteously; introduces a few grammatical and mechanical errors
Score 4	Formally provides information; addresses the intended audience	Uses an appropriate format for business letters; logically organizes most information	States the reasons for writing but needs more support for them; indicates central ideas or images	Uses formal language that somewhat acknowledges the nature of the relationship with the recipients; introduces some grammatical and mechanical errors
Score 3	Uses some informal language; does not clearly address the intended audience	Follows some formatting for formal business writing; organizes some information	Provides reasons for writing but lacks sufficient support for them; central ideas or images are unclear	Uses formal language that does not acknowledge the nature of the relationship with the recipients; introduces some grammatical and mechanical errors
Score 2	Uses informal language; does not address the intended audience appropriately	Follows some formatting for business writing; information often presented inconsistently or randomly	The reasons for writing are unclear and lack support; central ideas or images are limited	Uses informal language but communicates courteously; introduces many grammatical and mechanical errors
Score 1	Fails to communicate the letter's purpose; uses informal language; does not address the audience appropriately	Uses an inappropriate format for business writing; inconsistently or randomly presents information	Fails to state the reasons for writing; lacks central ideas or images	Uses informal language that does not communicate courteously; introduces numerous grammatical and mechanical errors that hinder reader understanding

Rubrics for Self-Assessment
Descriptive Essay

Evaluate your descriptive essay using one of the following rubrics:

Descriptive Essay—4-point rubric

	Audience and Purpose	Organization	Elaboration	Use of Language
Score 4	Contains details that work together to create a single, dominant impression of the topic	Is organized consistently, logically, and effectively	Contains creative use of sensory language	Contains sensory language that appeals to the five senses; contains no errors in grammar, punctuation, or spelling
Score 3	Creates through use of details a dominant impression of the topic	Is organized consistently	Contains much sensory language	Contains some sensory language; contains few errors in grammar, punctuation, and spelling
Score 2	Contains extraneous details that detract from the main impression	Is organized but not consistently	Contains some sensory language	Contains some sensory language, but it appeals to only one or two of the senses; contains some errors in grammar, punctuation, and spelling
Score 1	Contains details that are unfocused and create no dominant impression	Is disorganized and confusing	Contains no sensory language	Contains no sensory language; contains many errors in grammar, punctuation, and spelling

Descriptive Essay—5-point rubric

Criteria	Rating Scale				
	Not Very				Very
Focus: How clear is the impression you create of your subject?	1	2	3	4	5
Organization: How clearly and consistently is the description organized?	1	2	3	4	5
Support/Elaboration: How effectively are details used to create imagery?	1	2	3	4	5
Style: How effective is your use of figurative language?	1	2	3	4	5
Conventions: How well do the sensory details appeal to the five senses?	1	2	3	4	5

Descriptive Essay—6-point rubric

	Audience and Purpose	Organization	Elaboration	Use of Language
Score 6	Contains many sensory details that work together to create a single, dominant impression of the topic	Consistently presents a logical and effective organization	Vivid, sensory details support main idea; creative use of figurative language provides interesting comparisons	Contains vivid sensory language that strongly appeals to the five senses; very few errors in spelling, grammar, or punctuation
Score 5	Creates a strong main impression, supported with relevant sensory details	Presents a logical and effective organization	Sensory details strongly support main idea; contains figurative language that creates comparisons	Contains sensory language that appeals to the five senses; some errors in spelling, grammar, or punctuation, but they do not interfere with reader understanding
Score 4	Contains details that create a main impression of the topic	Presents most details in a suitable organization	Sensory details support main idea; figurative language used to create some comparisons	Contains some sensory language that appeals to the senses; errors in spelling, grammar, or punctuation may occur, but they do not interfere with reader understanding
Score 3	May create a main impression but does not adequately support it with sensory details	May have organization in some parts but lacks organization in other parts	Details in support of main idea not consistently effective; contains figurative language, but the comparisons are not fresh	Contains some sensory language, but it does not appeal to all of the senses; errors in spelling, grammar, or punctuation occasionally interfere with reader understanding
Score 2	Contains extraneous details that detract from the main impression	Very disorganized and not easy to follow	Limited use of sensory details in support of main idea; unsuccessful use of figurative language	Contains some sensory language, but it appeals to only one or two of the senses; errors in spelling, grammar, and punctuation hinder reader understanding
Score 1	Contains details that are unfocused or do not work in support of a clear main impression	Lacks organization and is confusing and difficult to follow; may be too brief to assess organization	No sensory details used in support of main idea; contains no figurative language	Contains no sensory language; many errors in spelling, grammar, and punctuation severely hinder reader understanding

Rubrics for Self-Assessment
Response to Literature

Evaluate your response to literature using one of the following rubrics:

Response to Literature—4-point rubric

	Audience and Purpose	Organization	Elaboration	Use of Language
Score 4	Presents sufficient background on the work(s); presents the writer's reactions forcefully	Presents points in a logical order, smoothly connecting them to the overall focus	Supports reactions and evaluations with elaborated reasons and well-chosen examples	Shows overall clarity and fluency; uses precise, evaluative words; makes few mechanical errors
Score 3	Presents background on the work(s); presents the writer's reactions clearly	Presents points in a logical order and connects them to the overall focus	Supports reactions and evaluations with specific reasons and examples	Shows good sentence variety; uses some precise evaluative terms; makes some mechanical errors
Score 2	Presents some background on the work(s); presents the writer's reactions at points	Organizes points poorly in places; connects some points to an overall focus	Supports some reactions and evaluations with reasons and examples	Uses awkward or overly simple sentence structures and vague evaluative terms; makes many mechanical errors
Score 1	Presents little or no background on the work(s); presents few, if any, of the writer's reactions	Presents information in a scattered and disorganized manner	Offers little support for reactions and evaluations	Presents incomplete thoughts; makes mechanical errors that cause confusion

Response to Literature—5-point rubric

Criteria	Rating Scale				
	Not Very				Very
Focus: How clear is your thesis statement?	1	2	3	4	5
Organization: How logical is your organization?	1	2	3	4	5
Support/Elaboration: How well do you use examples and quotations from the literary work?	1	2	3	4	5
Style: How well do you use your own ideas and experience to craft a personal response?	1	2	3	4	5
Conventions: How accurate are your references and citations to literary works?	1	2	3	4	5

Response to Literature—6-point rubric

	Audience and Purpose	Organization	Elaboration	Use of Language
Score 6	Clearly focuses on one aspect of the text, with sufficient summary information provided	Well organized, with strong transitions helping to link words and ideas	Develops any assertions with elaborated support and details from the text; provides the writer's reactions to the text	Varies sentence structures and makes good word choices; very few errors in spelling, grammar, or punctuation
Score 5	Focuses on one aspect of the text, with summary information provided	Clearly organized, although an occasional lapse may occur	Develops any assertions with support from the text; provides the writer's reactions to the text	Some sentence variety and good word choices; some errors in spelling, grammar, or punctuation, but they do not interfere with reader understanding
Score 4	Mainly focuses on one aspect of the text, with general summary information given	Is consistently organized, although perhaps simplistically	Adequate support for main idea is provided; provides some of the writer's reaction to the text	Sentence structures and word choices are appropriate; errors in spelling, grammar, or punctuation may occur, but they do not interfere with reader understanding
Score 3	Some summary information is given, but focus is not clear	May have organization in some parts but lacks organization in other parts	Support for the main idea is not fully developed; the writer's reaction may not be emphasized	Inconsistent control of sentence structures, and incorrect word choices; errors in spelling, grammar, or punctuation occasionally interfere with reader understanding
Score 2	An unsuccessful attempt is made to discuss the text; either topic is unclear or support is limited	Very disorganized and not easy to follow	Support is repetitive or undeveloped, with little discussion of the writer's reactions	Problematic sentence structures and frequent inaccuracies in word choices; errors in spelling, grammar, and punctuation hinder reader understanding
Score 1	Not fully engaged in the task; either the text is not discussed or no attempt is made to support ideas	Lacks organization and is confusing and difficult to follow; may be too brief to assess organization	Lacks support, summary information, or the writer's reactions	Little or no control over sentences and incorrect word choices may cause confusion; many errors in spelling, grammar, and punctuation severely hinder reader understanding

Rubrics for Self-Assessment
Writing for Assessment

Evaluate your writing for assessment using one of the following rubrics:

Writing for Assessment—4-point rubric

	Audience and Purpose	Organization	Elaboration	Use of Language
Score 4	Uses appropriately formal diction; clearly addresses writing prompt	Presents a clear and consistent organizational strategy	Provides several ideas to support the thesis; elaborates each idea; links all information to the thesis	Uses excellent sentence and vocabulary variety; includes very few mechanical errors
Score 3	Uses mostly formal diction; adequately addresses writing prompt	Presents a clear organizational strategy with few inconsistencies	Provides several ideas to support the thesis; elaborates most ideas with facts, details, or examples; links most information to the thesis	Uses adequate sentence and vocabulary variety; includes few mechanical errors
Score 2	Uses some informal diction; addresses writing prompt	Presents an inconsistent organizational strategy	Provides some ideas to support the thesis; does not elaborate some ideas; does not link some details to the thesis	Uses repetitive use of sentence structure and vocabulary; includes many mechanical errors
Score 1	Uses inappropriatel and informal diction; does not address writing prompt	Shows a lack of organizational strategy	Provides no thesis; does not elaborate ideas	Demonstrates poor use of language; generates confusion; includes many mechanical errors

Writing for Assessment—5-point rubric

Criteria	Rating Scale				
	Not Very				Very
Focus: How clearly is the writing prompt addressed?	1	2	3	4	5
Organization: How logical and consistent is the organization throughout the essay?	1	2	3	4	5
Support/Elaboration: How sufficiently do details support the thesis?	1	2	3	4	5
Style: How well do you avoid the mistakes of fragments and run-ons?	1	2	3	4	5
Conventions: How effectively is correct grammar, spelling, and punctuation used?	1	2	3	4	5

Writing for Assessment—6-point rubric

	Audience and Purpose	Organization	Elaboration	Use of Language
Score 6	Clearly addresses the writing prompt; a main idea is clearly presented	Well organized, with strong transitions helping to link words and ideas	The thesis is effectively developed with elaborated support and specific details and ideas	Varies sentence structures and makes good word choices; very few errors in spelling, grammar, or punctuation
Score 5	Clearly addresses the writing prompt; a main idea is presented	Clearly organized, although an occasional lapse may occur	The thesis is developed with elaborated support and details	Some sentence variety and good word choices; some errors in spelling, grammar, or punctuation, but they do not interfere with reader understanding
Score 4	Addresses the writing prompt; a main idea is presented	Is consistently organized, although perhaps simplistically	The thesis is adequately supported	Sentence structures and word choices are appropriate; errors in spelling, grammar, or punctuation may occur, but they do not interfere with reader understanding
Score 3	Although the prompt may be addressed, the main idea may not be clear	May have organization in some parts but lacks organization in other parts	The support given for the thesis may be unclear or undeveloped	Inconsistent control of sentence structures and incorrect word choices; errors in spelling, grammar, or punctuation occasionally interfere with reader understanding
Score 2	An attempt is made to address the prompt; however, either the topic is unclear or the support is limited	Very disorganized and not easy to follow	Limited support or support that does not substantiate a clear main idea	Problematic sentence structures and frequent inaccuracies in word choices; errors in spelling, grammar, and punctuation hinder reader understanding
Score 1	Little or on attempt is made to address the prompt; response is unfocused or undeveloped	Lacks organization and is confusing and difficult to follow; may be too brief to assess organization	Lacks elaboration of ideas	Little or no control over sentences and incorrect word choices may cause confusion; many errors in spelling, grammar, and punctuation severely hinder reader understanding

Rubrics for Self-Assessment
Comparison-and-Contrast Essay

Evaluate your comparison-and-contrast essay using one of the following rubrics:

Comparison-and-Contrast Essay—4-point rubric

	Audience and Purpose	Organization	Elaboration	Use of Language
Score 4	Clearly provides a reason for a comparison-and-contrast analysis	Clearly presents information in a consistent organization best suited to the topic	Elaborates several ideas with facts, details, or examples; links all information to comparison and contrast	Demonstrates excellent sentence and vocabulary variety; includes very few mechanical errors
Score 3	Adequately provides a reason for a comparison-and-contrast analysis	Presents information using an organization suited to the topic	Elaborates most ideas with facts, details, or examples; links most information to comparison and contrast	Demonstrates adequate sentence and vocabulary variety; includes few mechanical errors
Score 2	Provides a reason for a comparison-and-contrast analysis	Chooses an organization not suited to comparison and contrast	Does not elaborate all ideas; does not link some details to comparison and contrast	Demonstrates repetitive use of sentence structures and vocabulary; includes many mechanical errors
Score 1	Does not provide a reason for a comparison-and-contrast analysis	Shows a lack of organizational strategy	Does not provide facts or examples to support a comparison and contrast	Demonstrates poor use of language; generates confusion; includes many mechanical errors

Comparison-and-Contrast Essay—5-point rubric

Criteria	Rating Scale				
	Not Very				Very
Focus: How clear is the purpose for your comparison and contrast?	1	2	3	4	5
Organization: How logical is your organization for comparison?	1	2	3	4	5
Support/Elaboration: How well do you use evidence to support similarities and differences in your comparison?	1	2	3	4	5
Style: How smooth are the transitions between sentences and paragraphs?	1	2	3	4	5
Conventions: How correct is your grammar, especially your use of commas?	1	2	3	4	5

Comparison-and-Contrast Essay—6-point rubric

	Audience and Purpose	Organization	Elaboration	Use of Language
Score 6	Clearly presents a topic to be compared and contrasted and targets audience	Well organized, with strong transitions helping to link words and ideas	Effectively elaborates similarities and differences with details and examples as support	Varies sentence structures and makes good word choices; very few errors in spelling, grammar, or punctuation
Score 5	Provides a topic to be compared and contrasted and targets audience	Clearly organized, although an occasional lapse may occur	Elaborates similarities and differences with details and examples as support	Some sentence variety and good word choices; some errors in spelling, grammar, or punctuation, but they do not interfere with reader understanding
Score 4	Provides a topic to be compared and contrasted	Is consistently organized, although perhaps simplistically	Adequately addresses similarities and differences	Sentence structures and word choices are appropriate; errors in spelling, grammar, or punctuation may occur, but they do not interfere with reader understanding
Score 3	May attempt to compare and contrast two things but does not do so fully or clearly	May have organization in some parts but lacks organization in other parts	Does not consistently address similarities and differences; may emphasize some but neglect others	Inconsistent control of sentence structures and incorrect word choices; errors in spelling, grammar, or punctuation occasionally interfere with reader understanding
Score 2	Only a minimal attempt at comparing and contrasting two things; either topic is unclear or support is limited	Very disorganized and not easy to follow	Similarities and differences are not present or not well explained; support is minimal	Problematic sentence structures and frequent inaccuracies in word choices; errors in spelling, grammar, and punctuation hinder reader understanding
Score 1	Does not compare and contrast	Lacks organization and is confusing and difficult to follow; may be too brief to assess organization	Lacks support or elaboration	Little or no control over sentences and incorrect word choices may cause confusion; many errors in spelling, grammar, and punctuation severely hinder reader understanding

Rubrics for Self-Assessment
Summary

Evaluate your summary using one of the following rubrics:

Summary—4-point rubric

	Audience and Purpose	Organization	Elaboration	Use of Language
Score 4	Clearly and effectively expresses the deeper meaning of the work being summarized; demonstrates a clear awareness of both the audience and the purpose	Greatly enhances meaning; fully develops the central idea; includes support with significant details from the work	Includes the most essential details; clearly explains their significance and relevance to the central idea	Smoothly and effectively connects ideas with transitions; uses compelling language that is brief and precise
Score 3	Expresses a grasp of the deeper meaning of the work being summarized; demonstrates an awareness of the audience and the purpose	States the central idea; includes some important details with evidence from the work	Includes mostly essential details; somewhat explains their significance and relevance to the central idea	Connects ideas with transitions; uses language that is mostly brief and precise
Score 2	Expresses a limited sense of the deeper meaning of the work being summarized; demonstrates little understanding of the audience and the purpose	States the central idea somewhat vaguely; includes details from the work, but some may not be significant	Includes some random details that may or may not be significant; fails to explain their relevance to the central idea	Uses few transitions to connect ideas; uses language that is not brief and precise
Score 1	Fails to express the deeper meaning of the work being summarized; fails to demonstrate an understanding of the audience and the purpose	Fails to state the central idea; includes random details, most or all of which are insignificant	Fails to include significant details; fails to explain their relevance to the central idea	Fails to use transitions to connect ideas; uses language that is not brief and precise

Summary—5-point rubric

Criteria	Rating Scale				
	Not Very				Very
Focus: How well does the summary reflect the deeper meaning of the work?	1	2	3	4	5
Organization: How clear is the statement of the central idea?	1	2	3	4	5
Support/Elaboration: How significant are the details?	1	2	3	4	5
Style: How brief and precise is the writing?	1	2	3	4	5
Conventions: How effective are the transitions?	1	2	3	4	5

Summary—6-point rubric

	Audience and Purpose	Organization	Elaboration	Use of Language
Score 6	Clearly and effectively expresses the deeper meaning of the work being summarized; demonstrates a clear awareness of both the audience and the purpose	Greatly enhances meaning; fully develops the central idea; includes support with significant details from the work	Includes the most essential details; clearly explains their significance and relevance to the central idea	Smoothly and effectively connects ideas with transitions; uses compelling language that is brief and precise
Score 5	Expresses the deeper meaning of the work being summarized; demonstrates an awareness of the audience and the purpose	Develops the central idea; includes support with details from the work	Includes essential details; explains their significance and relevance to the central idea	Effectively connects ideas with transitions; uses language that is brief and precise
Score 4	Expresses a grasp of the deeper meaning of the work being summarized; demonstrates an awareness of the audience and the purpose	States the central idea; includes some important details from the work	Includes mostly essential details; explains somewhat their significance and relevance to the central idea	Connects ideas with transitions; uses language that is mostly brief and precise
Score 3	Expresses a limited sense of the deeper meaning of the work being summarized; demonstrates little understanding of the audience and the purpose	States the central idea somewhat vaguely; includes details from the work, but some may not be significant	Includes some inessential details; vaguely explains their significance and relevance to the central idea	Uses some transitions to connect ideas; uses language that is somewhat brief and precise
Score 2	Expresses little awareness of the deeper meaning of the work being summarized; indicates a lack of understanding of the audience and the purpose	States the central idea vaguely; includes some details, but many are insignificant	Includes random details that may or may not be significant; fails to explain their relevance to the central idea	Uses few transitions to connect ideas; uses language that is not brief and precise
Score 1	Fails to express the deeper meaning of the work being summarized; fails to demonstrate an understanding of the audience and the purpose	Fails to state the central idea; includes random details, most or all of which are insignificant	Fails to include significant details; fails to explain their relevance to the central idea	Fails to use transitions to connect ideas; uses language that is not brief and precise

Rubrics for Self-Assessment
Poem

Evaluate your poem using one of the following rubrics:

Poem—4-point rubric

	Rhythm and Other Sound Devices	Form and Pattern	Figurative Language and Imagery	Overall Effect
Score 4	Consistently conveys meaning through rhythm and other sound devices	Maintains form throughout; consistently uses patterns to emphasize words important to meaning	Consistently uses figurative language and imagery to convey thoughts and emotions	Powerfully synthesizes thought, experience, and emotion
Score 3	Occasionally conveys meaning through rhythm and other sound devices	Occasionally departs from form; occasionally uses patterns to emphasize words important to meaning	Generally uses figurative language and imagery to convey thoughts and emotions	Occasionally synthesizes thought, experience, and emotion
Score 2	Sporadically conveys meaning through rhythm and other sound devices; may lack rhythm or other sound devices to detriment of the poem	Addresses form or uses patterns but not to support meaning	Uses vague figurative language and imagery to convey thoughts or emotions	Communicates thought, experience, and emotion but does not show their synthesis
Score 1	Does not convey meaning through rhythm and other sound devices	Fails to use apparent form and pattern	Does not use figurative language and imagery or uses figurative language and imagery that clash with intended thoughts and emotions	Fails to communicate thought, experience, and emotion

Poem—5-point rubric

Criteria	Rating Scale				
	Not Very				Very
Rhythm and Other Sound Devices: How effectively do the sound devices convey the meaning, tone, and mood that you intend?	1	2	3	4	5
Form and Pattern: How consistent or helpful to the reader is the poem's organization?	1	2	3	4	5
Figurative Language and Imagery: How strong an impact do you make with figurative language and sensory details?	1	2	3	4	5
Overall Effect: How well do you synthesize thought, experience, and emotion?	1	2	3	4	5

Poem—6-point rubric

	Rhythm and Other Sound Devices	Form and Pattern	Figurative Language and Imagery	Overall Effect
Score 6	Consistently conveys meaning and directs emphasis through rhythm and other sound devices	Maintains form throughout; consistently uses patterns to emphasize words important to meaning	Consistently uses figurative language and imagery to convey thoughts and emotions	Powerfully synthesizes thought, experience, and emotion
Score 5	Generally conveys meaning and directs emphasis through rhythm and other sound devices	Generally maintains form; generally uses patterns to emphasize words important to meaning	Generally uses figurative language and imagery to convey thoughts and emotions	Generally synthesizes thought, experience, and emotion
Score 4	Occasionally conveys meaning and directs emphasis through rhythm and other sound devices	Occasionally departs from form; occasionally uses patterns to emphasize words important to meaning	Occasionally uses figurative language and imagery to convey thoughts and emotions	Occasionally synthesizes thought, experience, and emotion
Score 3	Sporadically conveys meaning or directs emphasis through rhythm or other sound devices	Only sporadically addresses form; only sporadically uses patterns to emphasize words important to meaning	Uses clichéd figurative language and imagery to convey thoughts and emotions	Provides a weak synthesis of thought, experience, and emotion
Score 2	Includes rhythm or other sound devices but not to support meaning; may lack rhythm or other sound devices to detriment of the poem	Addresses form or uses patterns but not to support meaning	Uses figurative language and imagery that clash with intended thoughts and emotions	Communicates thought, experience, and emotion but does not show their synthesis
Score 1	Does not convey meaning and does not direct emphasis through rhythm and other sound devices	Fails to use apparent form and pattern	Does not use figurative language or imagery to convey thoughts and emotion	Fails to communicate thought, experience, and emotion

Rubrics for Self-Assessment
Critique

Evaluate your critique using one of the following rubrics:

Critique—4-point rubric

	Audience and Purpose	Organization	Elaboration	Use of Language
Score 4	Provides arguments, illustrations, and diction that consistently target a specific audience; clearly projects knowledge of the subject and point of view	Presents points in a logical order; uses a clear and consistent organizational strategy	Successfully provides support and fully elaborates all key points of the critique	Shows overall clarity and fluency; presents very few mechanical errors
Score 3	Provides arguments, illustrations, and diction that adequately target a specific audience; projects knowledge of the subject and point of view	Presents points in order; uses a clear organizational strategy with occasional inconsistencies	Supports the main points of the critique with some elaboration	Demonstrates good sentence variety; presents some mechanical errors
Score 2	Provides some support that occasionally targets a specific audience; shows some knowledge of the subject and point of view	Organizes points poorly; uses an inconsistent organizational strategy	Provides some support of the critique but with little elaboration	Uses awkward or overly simple sentence structures; presents many mechanical errors
Score 1	Addresses no specific audience or purpose; shows little or no knowledge of the subject or point of view	Presents points in a scattered and disorganized manner; shows a lack of organizational strategy	Provides little, if any, relevant or reasonable support	Includes incomplete thoughts; presents many mechanical errors that cause confusion

Critique—5-point rubric

Criteria	Rating Scale				
	Not Very				Very
Focus: How clear is your purpose?	1	2	3	4	5
Organization: How consistent and logical is your organization?	1	2	3	4	5
Support/Elaboration: How well do you elaborate connections among ideas?	1	2	3	4	5
Style: How clear and fluent are your sentences?	1	2	3	4	5
Conventions: How correct is your use of spelling, grammar, and punctuation?	1	2	3	4	5

Critique—6-point rubric

	Audience and Purpose	Organization	Elaboration	Use of Language
Score 6	Provides arguments, illustrations, and diction that consistently target a specific audience; clearly projects knowledge of the subject and point of view	Presents points in a logical order; uses a clear and consistent organizational strategy	Successfully provides support and fully elaborates all key points of the critique	Shows overall clarity and fluency; presents very few mechanical errors
Score 5	Provides arguments, illustrations, and diction that mostly target a specific audience; projects knowledge of the subject and point of view	Presents points in a logical order; uses a clear organizational strategy with few inconsistencies	Supports and elaborates most key points of the critique	Shows sound sentence variety; presents few mechanical errors
Score 4	Provides arguments, illustrations, and diction that adequately target a specific audience; projects knowledge of the subject and point of view	Presents points in order; uses a clear organizational strategy with occasional inconsistencies	Supports the main points of the critique with some elaboration	Demonstrates good sentence variety; presents some mechanical errors
Score 3	Provides some support that occasionally targets a specific audience; shows some knowledge of the subject and point of view	Organizes some points; uses an inconsistent organizational strategy	Provides some support of the critique but with little elaboration	Demonstrates repetitive use of sentence structures; presents some mechanical errors
Score 2	Provides little support that targets a specific audience; shows limited knowledge of the subject and point of view	Organizes points poorly; uses an inconsistent organizational strategy	Provides little support of the critique; does not elaborate	Uses awkward or overly simple sentence structures; presents many mechanical errors
Score 1	Addresses no specific audience or purpose; shows little or no knowledge of the subject or point of view	Presents points in a scattered and disorganized manner; shows a lack of organizational strategy	Provides little, if any, relevant or reasonable support	Includes incomplete thoughts; presents many mechanical errors that cause confusion

Rubrics for Self-Assessment
Biographical Essay

Evaluate your biographical essay using one of the following rubrics:

Biographical Essay—4-point rubric

	Audience and Purpose	Organization	Elaboration	Use of Language
Score 4	Contains details that engage the audience; a main idea is clearly presented	Organizes events to create an interesting story; strong transitions help to link words and ideas	Contains rich details that shape vivid characters; contains dialogue that develops characters	Demonstrates excellent sentence and vocabulary variety; contains very few errors in spelling, grammar, or punctuation
Score 3	Contains some details that appeal to an audience; tells a complete story	Presents a clear sequence of events; has organization, although occasional lapses may occur	Contains details and dialogue that develop characters and describe setting but some vague words	Demonstrates adequate sentence and vocabulary variety; includes few errors in spelling, grammar, or punctuation
Score 2	Contains few details that appeal to an audience; attempts to tell a story but does not do so completely	Presents a confusing sequence of events; disorganized and not easy to follow	Contains limited details to develop characters or setting	Inconsistent control of sentence structures and vocabulary; includes many errors in spelling, grammar, or punctuation
Score 1	Is not written for a specific audience; little or no attempt is made to tell a story	Lacks organization and is confusing and difficult to follow	Contains few or no details to develop characters or setting; no dialogue is provided	Demonstrates poor use of language; creates confusion through errors in spelling, grammar, and punctuation

Biographical Essay—5-point rubric

Criteria	Rating Scale				
	Not Very				Very
Focus: How clear is your purpose?	1	2	3	4	5
Organization: How effectively organized is the sequence of events?	1	2	3	4	5
Support/Elaboration: How well developed are the characters and setting?	1	2	3	4	5
Style: How clear and fluent are your sentences?	1	2	3	4	5
Conventions: How accurate is your use of spelling, grammar, and punctuation?	1	2	3	4	5

Biographical Essay—6-point rubric

	Audience and Purpose	Organization	Elaboration	Use of Language
Score 6	Contains details that engage the audience; a main idea is clearly presented	Organizes events to create an interesting story; strong transitions help to link words and ideas	Contains rich details that shape vivid characters; makes effective use of dialogue that develops characters and plot	Demonstrates excellent sentence and vocabulary variety; contains very few errors in spelling, grammar, or punctuation
Score 5	Contains details appropriate for an audience; addresses a clear reason for writing	Presents a clear sequence of events; has suitable organization with transitions	Contains strong details with good use of dialogue; develops characters and describes setting	Demonstrates good sentence and vocabulary variety; contains few errors in spelling, grammar, or punctuation
Score 4	Contains some details that appeal to an audience; tells a complete story	Presents a sequence of events; has organization, although occasional lapses may occur	Contains details and dialogue that develop characters and describe setting but some vague words	Demonstrates adequate sentence and vocabulary variety; includes few errors in spelling, grammar, or punctuation
Score 3	Contains few details that appeal to an audience; attempts to tell a story but does not do so completely	Sequence of events has organization in some parts but lacks organization in other parts	Contains some details that develop characters; includes some use of dialogue	Inconsistent control of sentence structures and vocabulary; includes some errors in spelling, grammar, or punctuation
Score 2	Minimal attempt to tell a story; leaves purpose unclear	Presents a confusing sequence of events; disorganized and not easy to follow	Contains limited details to describe characters or setting	Uses awkward or overly simple sentence structures; includes many errors in spelling, grammar, and punctuation
Score 1	Is not written for a specific audience; little or no attempt is made to tell a story	Lacks organization and is confusing and difficult to follow	Contains few or no details to develop characters or setting; no dialogue is provided	Demonstrates poor use of language; creates confusion through errors in spelling, grammar, and punctuation

Rubrics for Self-Assessment
Reader Response Journal

Evaluate your reader response journal using one of the following rubrics:

Reader Response Journal—4-point rubric

	Audience and Purpose	Organization	Elaboration	Use of Language
Score 4	Connections are well explained and related to the text; reflections are discussed with much depth and detail	Consistently presents a logical and effective organization	Provides convincing, elaborated ideas with facts, details, and well-chosen examples	Incorporates many transitions to create clarity of expression; includes very few mechanical errors
Score 3	Connections are made, but some ideas need more detail and explanation	Uses a clear organizational strategy with occasional inconsistencies	Elaborates ideas with facts, details, and examples; links most information to the text	Incorporates some transitions to connect ideas; includes some mechanical errors
Score 2	A connection is made, but no explanation is given; reflection is lacking or not related to the text with examples	Presents an inconsistent organizational strategy	Does not elaborate most ideas; does not link information to the text	Incorporates few transitions; does not connect ideas well; includes many mechanical errors
Score 1	No personal response or reflection is made	Demonstrates a lack of organizational strategy	Offers no support or elaboration	Does not connect ideas; includes many mechanical errors that hinder reader understanding

Reader Response Journal—5-point rubric

Criteria	Rating Scale				
	Not Very				Very
Focus: How clear is your purpose?	1	2	3	4	5
Organization: How consistent and logical is your organization?	1	2	3	4	5
Support/Elaboration: How well do you elaborate connections among ideas?	1	2	3	4	5
Style: How clear and fluent are your sentences?	1	2	3	4	5
Conventions: How correct is your use of spelling, grammar, and punctuation?	1	2	3	4	5

Reader Response Journal—6-point rubric

	Audience and Purpose	Organization	Elaboration	Use of Language
Score 6	Connections are well explained and related to the text; reflections are discussed with much depth and detail	Consistently presents a logical and effective organization	Provides convincing, elaborated ideas with facts, details, and well-chosen examples	Incorporates many transitions to create clarity of expression; includes very few mechanical errors
Score 5	Connections are made; reflections are supported with clear evidence from the work	Presents a clear organizational strategy with a few inconsistencies	Elaborates most ideas with facts, details, and examples; links most information to the text	Effectively uses transitions to help flow of ideas; includes few mechanical errors
Score 4	Some connections are made, but ideas need more detail and explanation	Uses a clear organizational strategy with occasional inconsistencies	Elaborates several ideas with facts, details, and examples	Incorporates some transitions to connect ideas; includes some mechanical errors
Score 3	A connection is made, but little explanation is given; reaction or reflection is lacking in detail	May have organization in some parts but lacks organization elsewhere	Provides some support but with little elaboration	Incorporates few transitions; does not connect ideas well; includes many mechanical errors
Score 2	Reflection is lacking or not related to the text with examples; makes no connection to text	Presents an inconsistent organizational strategy	Does not elaborate most ideas; does not link information to the text	Uses few, if any transitions to connect ideas; includes many mechanical errors
Score 1	No personal response or reflection is made	Demonstrates a lack of organizational strategy	Offers no support or elaboration	Does not connect ideas; includes many mechanical errors that hinder reader understanding

Rubrics for Self-Assessment
Generic (Holistic) Writing

Evaluate your writing assignment using one of the following rubrics:

Generic (Holistic) Writing—4-point rubric

	Audience and Purpose	Organization	Elaboration	Use of Language
Score 4	Consistently focuses on purpose for writing and offers fresh insights; consistently targets an audience through word choices and supporting details	Consistently presents information in an appropriate and easy-to-follow progression	Provides convincing, well-developed support for ideas	Displays an original voice; shows mature sentence structures and variety; contains very few mechanical errors
Score 3	Identifies purpose for writing; generally targets an audience through word choices and supporting details	Generally presents information in an appropriate and easy-to-follow progression	Provides some support and development for ideas	Occasionally displays an original voice; some sentence variety and effective word choices; contains some mechanical errors
Score 2	Occasionally loses focus on purpose or goes off topic; only sporadically targets an audience	Occasionally loses track of direction and becomes difficult to follow	Does not elaborate all ideas; provides illogical support for some ideas	Only sporadically displays an original voice; uses overly simple or unvarying sentence structures; contains many mechanical errors
Score 1	Does not identify purpose for writing; does not address a clearly defined audience or inappropriately addresses audience	Presents information in a disconnected and difficult-to-follow manner	Does not develop ideas; may repeat but not build on ideas	Fails to carry a voice; shows a lack of sentence sense; contains many mechanical errors that hinder reader understanding

Generic (Holistic) Writing—5-point rubric

Criteria	Rating Scale				
	Not Very				Very
Focus: How clear is your purpose for writing? How consistent is your attention to an audience?	1	2	3	4	5
Organization: How easy is your writing to follow from sentence to sentence and from paragraph to paragraph?	1	2	3	4	5
Support/Elaboration: How well do you develop your ideas?	1	2	3	4	5
Style: How noticeable is your personal voice? How mature and varied are your sentences?	1	2	3	4	5
Conventions: How accurate is your spelling, grammar, and punctuation?	1	2	3	4	5

Generic (Holistic) Writing—6-point rubric

	Audience and Purpose	Organization	Elaboration	Use of Language
Score 6	Consistently maintains focus on purpose for writing and offers fresh insights; consistently targets and shows sensitivity to an audience through word choices and supporting details	Consistently presents information in an appropriate and easy-to-follow progression	Consistently provides convincing, well-developed support for ideas	Displays an original voice; shows mature sentence structures and variety; contains very few mechanical errors
Score 5	Generally focuses on purpose for writing and offers fresh insights; targets an audience through word choices and supporting details	Generally presents information in an appropriate and easy-to-follow progression	Generally provides convincing, well-developed support for ideas	Generally displays an original voice; generally shows mature sentence structures and variety; contains few mechanical errors
Score 4	Identifies purpose for writing and offers insights; generally targets an audience through word choice and supporting details	Presents information in an appropriate progression, though lapses may occur	Provides some support and development for ideas	Occasionally displays an original voice; shows some mature sentence structures and variety; contains some mechanical errors
Score 3	Occasionally loses focus on purpose; only sporadically targets an audience through word choices and supporting details	Occasionally loses track of direction and becomes difficult to follow	Does not elaborate all ideas; provides illogical support for some ideas	Only sporadically displays an original voice; sporadically shows mature sentence structures and variety; contains several mechanical errors
Score 2	Confuses purpose for writing; obscures or misses audience in word choices and supporting details	Lacks transitions and other connections between sentences and between paragraphs	Provides inadequate or illogical support for ideas	Fails to carry an original voice; uses overly simple or unvarying sentence structures; contains many mechanical errors
Score 1	Does not identify purpose for writing; does not address a clearly defined audience or inappropriately addresses audience	Presents information in a disconnected and difficult-to-follow manner	Does not develop ideas; may repeat but not build on ideas	Fails to carry a voice; shows a lack of sentence sense; contains many mechanical errors that hinder reader understanding

Rubric for Analyzing Persuasive Techniques

Use the following rubric to assess analyzing persuasive techniques.

Rating System

+ = excellent	✓ = average	— = weak

Content

Recognizes purpose _____

Develops expectations _____

Categorizes persuasive speech according to type _____

Assesses appropriateness of evidence _____

Assesses pertinence of proof _____

Analyzes reasoning for flaws and weaknesses _____

Delivery

Interprets and evaluates presentation strategies _____

Critiques diction and syntax in relation to purpose _____

Identifies logical fallacies _____

Listens critically for clarity, quality, effectiveness, and general coherence _____

Listens critically for emotional appeals, rhetorical questions, and deductive arguments _____

Analyzes the techniques used for the particular audience _____

Analysis Summary

The types of persuasive techniques are identified and evaluated _____

Logical fallacies are taken into account _____

An evaluation of clarity, quality, effectiveness, and general coherence is made _____

Sound reasoning is used to make a judgment about the persuasive techniques _____

Rubric for Critiquing Persuasive Arguments

Use the following rubric to assess critiquing persuasive arguments.

Rating System		
+ = excellent	**✓ = average**	**— = weak**

Content
Analyzes persuasive techniques _____
Identifies use of attack *ad hominem*, false causality, and red herring _____
Evaluates techniques used in oral addresses _____
Challenges generalizations _____

Delivery
Recognizes argument structure _____
Listens critically to the organization of ideas _____
Listens critically for persuasive devices and fallacious arguments _____
Identifies circular reasoning, overgeneralization, and bandwagon effect _____
Listens critically for diction and syntax in relation to the purpose of the argument _____

Critique Summary
The argument is broken down into parts for analysis _____
A decision is made as to whether the argument is accurate or faulty _____
A decision is made as to whether the argument is strong or weak _____
An evaluation of clarity, quality, effectiveness, and general coherence is made _____
Sound reasoning is used to critique the argument _____

Rubric for Analyzing Advertising

Use the following rubric to assess analyzing advertising.

Rating System

| + = excellent | ✓ = average | — = weak |

Content

Recognizes the persuasive message and techniques used to present it _____

Identifies the type of media used to convey the persuasive message _____

Identifies purpose of the message and determines the targeted audience _____

Delivery

Identifies advertising elements such as concept, hook, charged language, characters, special effects, and mood _____

Assesses purpose and impact of advertising elements _____

Identifies and assesses cultural values illustrated in the advertisement _____

Evaluates individual visual elements for appropriateness and contributing factors _____

Analysis Summary

Tone, image, cultural values, and purpose are taken into account _____

A decision as to whether the advertisement's purpose had been achieved is made _____

An overall conclusion is drawn about the advertisement _____

Rubric for Media Analysis of the News

Use the following rubric to evaluate media analyses of the news.

Content
Analyzes explicit influences _____
Analyzes implicit influences _____
Identifies editorials _____
Recognizes opinion forums _____
Questions sources of information _____
Weighs objectivity and subjectivity _____

Delivery
Analyzes structure _____
Considers the impact of the story's placement in a broadcast _____
Considers omissions and inclusions of information _____
Compares new sources _____
Evaluates timeliness of news coverage _____

Analysis Summary
Media sources are analyzed _____
Information is interpreted _____
The media's communication methods are analyzed _____
Sound reasoning is used to make a judgment about the news conveyed and the
media's influence _____

Rubric for Interview Techniques

Use the following rubric to evaluate interview techniques

Rating System

+ = excellent	✓ = average	— = weak

Content

Learns about the job and company _____

Prepares to ask questions _____

Establishes and maintains context _____

Uses language that conveys maturity, sensitivity, and respect _____

Reviews information gained from interview questions and responses _____

Delivery

Demonstrates knowledge of the person or organization _____

Responds correctly and effectively to questions _____

Makes notes on information gained and responses to concerns and issues _____

Demonstrates knowledge of the subject or organization _____

Interview Summary

Attitude toward interview is apparent and appropriate _____

Attitude toward the interviewer is apparent and appropriate _____

Relevant questions are asked of the interviewer _____

Full and precise responses are given to the interviewer's questions _____

An active role in the interview is taken _____

The effectiveness of the interview is evaluated _____

Rubric for Delivering an Autobiographical Presentation

Use the following rubric to evaluate autobiographical presentations.

Rating System		
+ = excellent	✓ = average	— = weak

Content

Establishes and maintains context _____

Uses elements such as rhetorical questions, parallel structure, concrete images, figurative language, characterization, irony, and dialogue _____

Illustrates personal relationship to the story _____

Draws a conclusion _____

Delivery

Uses appropriate verbal techniques _____

Uses appropriate nonverbal techniques _____

Uses an organizational structure that matches purpose _____

Use sound or visual effects, graphics, and background music to enhance or complement the presentation _____

Achieves a focused and coherent presentation _____

Presentation Summary

Attitude toward presentation is apparent and appropriate _____

Attitude toward the audience is apparent and appropriate _____

Preparation is evident and thorough _____

Organization is discernible and effective _____

Rubric for Delivering a Persuasive Speech

Use the following rubric to evaluate persuasive speeches.

Rating System

+ = excellent	✓ = average	— = weak

Content

Establishes and maintains context _____

Uses a basic type of persuasive speech: proposition of fact, value, problem, or policy _____

Distinguishes between and uses logical arguments, such as inductive and deductive reasoning or syllogisms and analogies _____

Modifies content to fit the audience's knowledge _____

Delivery

Uses appropriate verbal techniques _____

Uses appropriate nonverbal techniques _____

Uses an organizational structure that matches purpose _____

Uses logical, ethical, and emotional appeals that enhance the selected tone and purpose _____

Achieves a focused and coherent presentation _____

Presentation Summary

Attitude toward speech is apparent and appropriate _____

Attitude toward the audience is apparent and appropriate _____

Effective persuasive techniques are used _____

Preparation is evident and thorough _____

Organization is discernible and effective _____

Rubric for Presenting an Oral Response to Literature

Use the following rubric to evaluate oral responses to literature.

Rating System

+ = excellent   ✓ = average   — = weak

Content

Advances a judgment that demonstrates a grasp of the work's significant ideas _____

Supports ideas and viewpoints through references to the text or to other works _____

Demonstrates awareness of the author's use of stylistic devices _____

Assesses the ambiguities, nuances, and complexities within the text _____

Presents a strong introduction and conclusion _____

Delivery

Uses appropriate verbal techniques _____

Uses appropriate nonverbal techniques _____

Chooses and maintains a logical organization _____

Concisely summarizes the main ideas of the text _____

Uses evocative language that is clear and unambiguous _____

Engages listeners _____

Presentation Summary

Attitude toward the piece of literature is apparent and appropriate _____

Attitude toward the audience is apparent and appropriate _____

Preparation is evident and thorough _____

Organization is discernible and effective _____

Rubric for Presenting a Proposal

Use the following rubric to evaluate presenting a proposal.

Rating System

+ = excellent	✓ = average	— = weak

Content

Establishes and maintains context _____

Identifies the need for action _____

States a clear position regarding a course of action _____

Arranges details, descriptions, and examples persuasively _____

Delivery

Uses appropriate verbal techniques _____

Uses appropriate nonverbal techniques _____

Organizes and presents the proposal effectively _____

Focuses on the audience _____

Addresses background and interests of the audience _____

Achieves a focused and coherent presentation _____

Presentation Summary

Attitude toward the needed action is appropriate _____

Attitude toward the audience is apparent and appropriate _____

Preparation is evident and thorough _____

Organization is discernible and effective _____

Rubric for Delivering a Research Presentation

Use the following rubric to evaluate research presentations.

Rating System

+ = excellent	✓ = average	— = weak

Content
Establishes and maintains context _____
Poses a concise question on a relevant topic _____
Addresses the topic completely and thoroughly _____
Draws from multiple authoritative sources _____
Supports the topic with facts, details, examples, and explanations _____
Cites reference sources appropriately _____

Delivery
Uses appropriate verbal techniques _____
Uses appropriate nonverbal techniques _____
Uses an organizational structure that matches purpose and information _____
Presents appropriate visual aids _____
Achieves a focused and coherent presentation _____
Answers questions from the audience appropriately _____

Presentation Summary
Attitude toward topic is apparent and appropriate _____
Clear and accurate perspectives are conveyed _____
Attitude toward the audience is apparent and appropriate _____
Preparation is evident and thorough _____
Organization is discernible and effective _____

Alternative Assessment

Name _____ Date _____

Reading Strategy Inventory

Directions: Use this inventory to help you analyze your reading habits and set goals for yourself. Think carefully about each question and answer honestly. Keep these pages for future reference. At the end of the year, you can use them to assess your progress and set new goals.

1. Which of the following strategies do you use *before* you read? Circle the word that best describes your habits.

I preview the material by thinking about the title, reviewing any pictures, and reading the introduction and similar material.   never   sometimes   always

I give myself a purpose for reading, such as deciding what I expect to learn about the theme and how it relates to me personally.   never   sometimes   always

I recall what I already know about the subject about which I plan to read.   never   sometimes   always

2. Which of the following strategies do you use *while* you read? Circle the word that best describes your habits.

I try to predict what will happen and change my prediction as I read further.   never   sometimes   always

I ask questions about what is happening, why characters act as they do, or why the author chose to include particular details or to use certain words.   never   sometimes   always

I visualize the characters and events.   never   sometimes   always

I compare characters to myself or to people I know.   never   sometimes   always

3. Which of the following strategies do you use *after* you read? Circle the word that best describes your habits.

I respond to what I have read by discussing it with someone.   never   sometimes   always

I review my predictions and questions to determine if my predictions were correct and my questions were answered.   never   sometimes   always

I use what I have learned in a future project or activity.   never   sometimes   always

4. Put a check mark beside the responses that describe what you do when you encounter these problems. You may check more than one response. You may also add additional responses.

When I come across an unfamiliar word, I

_____ try to figure out its meaning from the way it is used.

_____ consult a dictionary.

_____ ignore it and hope it will become clear as I read further.

When I do not understand the meaning of a sentence, I

_____ read the sentence several times.

_____ read the other sentences in the paragraph several times.

_____ ignore the sentence and hope it will become clear as I read.

When I want to remember important information I have read in subjects such as science and social studies, I

_____ ask myself questions about the important ideas.

_____ relate the information to something I already know.

_____ repeat the information to myself several times.

_____ take notes.

When I read an entire passage over again, it is usually because

_____ I do not understand it.

_____ it seemed important to remember that particular passage.

_____ I want to summarize it for myself.

When reading a textbook, I

_____ read faster or slower depending on the difficulty of the material.

_____ skip parts I do not understand.

_____ make predictions about what I am reading.

When reading a textbook, I assume that

_____ all the sentences are important or they would not be there.

_____ some sentences are more important than others.

_____ sentences with the most details are the most important sentences.

Review your answers to the previous questions regarding your reading interests and strategies. Then, set goals for yourself by answering the following questions.

5. My greatest strength in reading is _____
_____
_____
_____
_____
_____ .

6. One thing I need to improve about my reading is _____
_____
_____
_____
_____
_____ .

7. A strategy I should use more often when reading is _____
_____
_____
_____
_____
_____ .

8. In addition to assigned reading, I plan to read at least _____
_____
_____
_____
_____ .

9. I want to broaden my reading interests by reading more _____
_____
_____
_____
_____
_____ .

Name _____ Date _____

Preparing to Read

Directions: Use these two sets of questions to help you prepare to read a selection and to assess the results of your reading.

Title _____ Author _____

Before I Read

1. What type of selection is this? _____

2. Why am I reading this? _____
   _____

3. What do the title, pictures, and general appearance of the selection suggest about the subject or theme?
   _____
   _____

4. What do I know that might help me better understand this selection?
   _____
   _____

5. What do I know about the author and his/her style? Have I read other works by this author?
   _____
   _____

6. How might the theme or subject of this selection relate to my own life and experiences?
   _____
   _____

7. I expect this selection will provide (circle one or more)

   information   instruction   pleasure   other

   because _____

8. I expect this to be (circle one)

   easy   average   challenging

   reading because
   _____

9. What other things can I predict about the selection? What other questions do I have about it?

_____

_____

_____

_____

After I Read

1. How accurate were my predictions or expectations? Did any questions go unanswered? Which ones?

_____

_____

_____

2. What part of the selection was the most informative or enjoyable?

_____

_____

_____

3. What part was the most troublesome or difficult?

_____

_____

_____

4. What elements provoked the strongest response? Why?

_____

_____

_____

5. What did I already know that helped me as I read?

_____

_____

_____

6. What is the most important thing I learned from reading this selection?

_____

_____

_____

Name _____ Date _____

Independent Reading Guide: The Novel

Directions: Use the following questions to clarify your understanding of and response to a novel. Reflect on each question before answering. If you are keeping a *Reader's Response Journal* or wish to start one, use one of the suggested activities to make an entry.

Novel Title _____ Author _____

Elements of the Novel

1. Who is the protagonist—the main character—in the novel?
   _____

2. What kind of person is the protagonist? _____

3. What evidence in the novel leads me to this opinion of the protagonist?
   _____

4. What challenge or conflict does the protagonist encounter? _____

5. How is the conflict resolved? _____
   _____

6. What other important characters are involved in the conflict? _____
   _____

7. What is the setting of this novel? _____

8. Who tells the story—one of the characters or an outside observer?
   _____

9. What event do I consider to be the climax of the novel? _____
   _____

10. How would I describe the mood? How does the author establish that mood?
    _____
    _____

11. State the theme or central idea of this novel. _____
    _____
    _____

12. Is there a sentence or short passage that states or strongly implies the theme? If so, what is it?

_____

_____

Response to the Novel

Rate this novel by circling the appropriate word.

13. The characters and dialogue are believable.	weak	fair	strong
14. The plot engages my interest.	weak	fair	strong
15. This novel is written in a style that is clear and interesting.	weak	fair	strong
16. The details in this novel add to its appeal.	weak	fair	strong
17. Overall, I rate this novel as	weak	fair	strong

Reasons for my rating: _____

_____

_____

18. What predictions and questions occurred to me as I read this story? Were my predictions accurate? Were my questions answered?

_____

_____

_____

_____

Reader's Response Journal

- Is there a character in this novel that you have strong feelings about? Explain your feelings. Does this character remind you of someone you know? If so, in what way? Did your feelings about this character change as the story progressed?

- Is there one event in this novel that was surprising or confusing? If so, write a brief paragraph to the author expressing your thoughts.

Name _____ Date _____

Independent Reading Guide: The Short Story

Directions: Use the following questions to clarify your understanding of and response to a short story. Reflect on each question before answering. If you are keeping a *Reader's Response Journal* or wish to start one, use one of the suggested activities to make an entry.

Story Title _____ Author _____

Elements of the Short Story

1. Who is the protagonist—the main character—in the story?

_____

2. What challenge or conflict does the protagonist encounter? _____

_____

3. How is the conflict resolved? _____

_____

4. What other important characters are involved in the conflict? _____

_____

5. What kind of person is the protagonist? _____

_____

6. What evidence in the story leads me to this opinion of the protagonist?

_____

_____

7. Where does this story take place? _____

_____

8. How would I describe the mood? How does the author establish this mood?

_____

_____

_____

_____

9. Summarize the theme or central idea of this short story. _____

_____

10. Is there a sentence or short passage that states or strongly implies the theme?
If so, what is it?

_____

_____

Response to the Short Story

Rate this short story by circling the appropriate word.

11. The characters and dialogue are believable, and the plot engages my interest.	weak	fair	strong
12. This story is written in a style that is clear and interesting.	weak	fair	strong
13. This story helps me understand people and events.	weak	fair	strong
14. The details in this story could be easily visualized as I read.	weak	fair	strong
15. Overall, I rate this story as	weak	fair	strong

Reasons for my rating: _____

_____

_____

_____

_____

_____

Reader's Response Journal

- What predictions and questions occurred to me as I read this story? Were my predictions accurate? Were my questions answered?

- In a short paragraph, describe an element of the short story that reminds you of something in your own life.

Name _____ Date _____

Independent Reading Guide: The Play

Directions: Use the following questions to clarify your understanding of and response to a play. Reflect on each question before answering. If you are keeping a *Reader's Response Journal* or wish to start one, use one of the suggested activities to make an entry.

Play Title _____ Author _____

Elements of the Play

1. Who is the protagonist—the main character—in the play? _____

2. What kind of person is the protagonist? _____

   _____

3. What evidence in the play leads me to this opinion of the protagonist?

   _____

   _____

4. What challenge or conflict does the protagonist encounter? _____

   _____

5. How is the conflict resolved? _____

   _____

   _____

6. What other important characters are involved in the conflict? _____

   _____

7. Where and when does this play take place? How does the playwright reveal this information?

   _____

   _____

8. How would I describe the mood? How does the playwright establish this mood?

   _____

   _____

   _____

9. Summarize the theme or central idea of this play. What other books or plays with this theme have I read?

_____

_____

10. Is there a short passage or a dialogue that states or strongly implies the theme? If so, what is it?

_____

_____

Response to the Play

Rate this play by circling the appropriate word.

11.	The characters and dialogue are believable.	weak	fair	strong
12.	The stage directions and the action of the characters are easily visualized.	weak	fair	strong
13.	The plot of the play engages my interest.	weak	fair	strong
14.	This play helps me understand people and events.	weak	fair	strong
15.	This play evokes strong feelings or thoughts about the message or the characters.	weak	fair	strong
16.	Reading this play increases my interest in seeing a performance of the play.	weak	fair	strong
17.	Overall, I rate this play as	weak	fair	strong

Reasons for my rating: _____

_____

_____

_____

Reader's Response Journal

- What predictions and questions occurred to me as I read this play? Were my predictions accurate? Were my questions answered?

- Briefly describe a character or a scene in this play that reminds you of someone you know or an experience in your life.

Independent Reading Guide: Nonfiction

Directions: Use the following questions to clarify your understanding of and response to a nonfiction selection. Reflect on each question before answering. If you are keeping a *Reader's Response Journal* or wish to start one, use one of the suggested activities to make an entry.

Title _____ Author _____

Circle the type of nonfiction.

essay	biography	autobiography	sports	how-to
humor	letter	memoir	careers	astronomy
history	article	geography	personal narrative	

other _____

This nonfiction selection (circle one or more)

    instructs   informs   describes   persuades   entertains.

This nonfiction selection tells about (circle one or more)

    person(s)   place(s)   thing(s)   event(s)   other: _____.

Elements of Nonfiction

1. Who or what is this nonfiction selection about? _____
   _____

2. What is the author's purpose for writing this selection? _____
   _____

3. What information, facts, or examples does the author include to support the
   purpose? _____
   _____

4. For what group of people would this selection be most appealing? What does
   the author include to appeal to this audience? _____
   _____

5. What technique(s) does the author use to appeal to the reader? Circle one and
   give an example from the selection.

description	argument	comparison and contrast
emotional language	quotations	personal recollections

   Example: _____

6. Summarize the theme or central idea of this selection.

_____

_____

7. Is there a sentence or short passage that states or strongly implies the message or main idea? If so, what is it?

_____

_____

Response to the Nonfiction Selection

Rate this nonfiction selection by circling the appropriate word.

8. This selection is written in a style that is clear and interesting.   weak   fair   strong

9. The topic, main idea, or purpose is obvious.   weak   fair   strong

10. The details are helpful, informative, and understandable.   weak   fair   strong

11. I can connect with the author's thoughts or feelings about the subject.   weak   fair   strong

12. This selection helps me understand people and events.   weak   fair   strong

13. Overall, I rate this nonfiction selection as   weak   fair   strong

Reasons for my rating: _____

_____

14. What predictions and questions occurred to me as I read this selection? Were my predictions accurate? Were my questions answered?

_____

_____

Reader's Response Journal

• Describe something that you learned from reading this selection. Write about it and explain its significance.

• What do you think is this author's greatest strength as a writer? Write a short paragraph to explain your reason and give an example from the selection to support your reason.

Name _____ Date _____

Independent Reading Guide: Poetry

Directions: Use the following questions to clarify your understanding of and response to a poem. Reflect on each question before answering. If you are keeping a *Reader's Response Journal* or wish to start one, use one of the suggested activities to make an entry.

Poem Title _____ Poet _____

Circle the literary techniques the poet uses in this poem.

     simile   metaphor   personification   rhyme

     repetition   onomatopoeia   alliteration   other_____

In this poem, the poet is attempting to (circle one or more)

     tell a story   create an image

     express a feeling or emotion   other_____.

Elements of the Poem

1. Give an example of a literary technique used by the poet. _____
   _____

2. Is the poem written in stanzas? If so, how many? _____

3. How would I describe the rhythm of the poem? _____

4. Does the rhythm seem to match the message or meaning of the poem?
   Explain. _____
   _____
   _____

5. How would I describe the mood of the poem? How does the poet establish
   this mood? _____
   _____
   _____

6. What do I think the poet wants me to know, feel, value, or believe?
   _____
   _____
   _____

7. Does a particular word or phrase carry important meaning for the poem? If so, which word or phrase and what meaning does it convey?

_____

_____

Response to the Poem

Rate this poem by circling the appropriate word.

8. The words appeal to my sense of sight, hearing, touch, taste, or smell. weak   fair   strong

9. The meaning of this poem is clear and precise. weak   fair   strong

10. I can feel the rhythm of the poem as I read it. weak   fair   strong

11. I can easily connect the feelings or events in this poem with my own experiences. weak   fair   strong

12. Overall, I rate this poem as weak   fair   strong

Reasons for my rating: _____

_____

13. What qualities did I like or dislike about this poem? Why? _____

_____

_____

14. What predictions and questions occurred to me as I read this poem? Were my predictions accurate? Were my questions answered?

_____

_____

Reader's Response Journal

- When you reread the poem, did you discover something that was not obvious from your first reading? Explain your discovery and the reason it may have occurred.

- Copy a phrase, line, or passage from the poem and then write a brief comment describing your feelings or thoughts about the passage.

Name _____ Date _____

Independent Reading Guide: Myths and Folk Tales

Directions: Use the following questions to clarify your understanding of and response to a myth, folktale, fable, or legend. Reflect on each question before answering. If you are keeping a *Reader's Response Journal* or wish to start one, use one of the suggested activities to make an entry.

Title _____ Author _____

Circle the type of selection.

        fable   myth   folk tale   legend

Circle one or more phrases that describe this selection.

    Tells about events in nature

    Explains how certain creatures came into being

    Teaches a moral lesson

    Stresses admirable behaviors or ideals

    Expresses a generalization

    Uses a symbol to stand for an idea

    Centers around a conflict

    Expresses an idea common to many people

Elements of the Myth, Folk Tale, Fable, or Legend

1. When and where does this story take place? _____
_____

2. Of what importance is the setting to the story, if any? _____
_____

3. Who are the main characters? _____

4. How would I describe the characters? What are their outstanding qualities?
_____
_____

5. What challenge or conflict do the characters encounter? _____
_____

6. How is the conflict resolved? _____
_____

7. What cultural value, belief, idea, or custom is this selection about?

   _____

8. Summarize the theme, central idea, or message of this selection.

   _____

9. Is there a sentence or short passage that states or strongly implies the theme, central idea, or message? If so, what is it?

   _____

   _____

Response to the Myth, Folk Tale, Fable, or Legend

Rate this selection by circling the appropriate word.

10. This selection is written in a style that is clear and interesting.	weak	fair	strong
11. This selection engages my interest.	weak	fair	strong
12. The message of this selection is obvious.	weak	fair	strong
13. The message is worthwhile for today's culture.	weak	fair	strong
14. Overall, I rate this selection as	weak	fair	strong

   Reasons for my rating: _____

   _____

15. Does this selection remind me of other selections I have read? If so, in what way? _____

   _____

16. What predictions and questions occurred to me as I read this story? Were my predictions accurate? Were my questions answered?

   _____

   _____

Reader's Response Journal

- After a careful rereading of the story, write a new ending for the story and include a new message or lesson if one is required.

- Does this story remind you of an experience or event in your life? Briefly tell how the experience relates to the story.

Name _____ Date _____

Initial Self-Assessment: Writing

Directions: This self-assessment is designed to help you recall the types of writing you have done, consider your strengths and weaknesses, and set goals for yourself. Answer each question or complete each statement honestly and keep it for future reference. At the end of the year, you can review this assessment and set new goals.

1. I have experience writing the following types of papers:

   _____ **Personal Expression** Expressing your thoughts, feelings, or experiences

   _____ **Description** Creating a picture of how something looks, sounds, feels, smells, or tastes

   _____ **Narration** Telling a true or fictional story

   _____ **Exposition: Giving Information** Providing information or explaining something to a reader

   _____ **Exposition: Making Connections** Comparing and contrasting, offering solutions to a problem, or explaining an opinion

   _____ **Persuasion** Trying to convince a reader to agree with you

   _____ **Reports** Summarizing the results of research

   _____ **Creative Writing** Expressing your personal views through imaginative writing like poetry

   _____ **Responses to Literature** Presenting your ideas and feelings about something you have read

2. Of the types of writing I have done, the type I am best at is _____
   _____.

3. The reasons I am good at this type of writing are _____
   _____
   _____
   _____.

4. Of the types of writing I have done, the type I have the most trouble with is
   _____.

5. The reason I have trouble with this type of writing is _____
   _____.

6. I would like to try more of the following types of writing: _____
   _____.

7. I perform the following steps when I write (circle the word that applies):

Use a journal, brainstorming, or a similar method for deciding on a topic.	never	occasionally	always
Think carefully about the audience for which I am writing.	never	occasionally	always
Write down my purpose for writing before beginning a first draft.	never	occasionally	always
Write a draft without stopping to correct spelling and mechanical problems.	never	occasionally	always
Ask someone else to read my draft before revising.	never	occasionally	always
Proofread and correct mechanical spelling errors after the draft has been revised.	never	occasionally	always
Try to make my final copy neat and attractive.	never	occasionally	always

8. The step in the writing process I do best is _____
_____
_____
_____ .

9. The reason I am particularly good at this is _____
_____
_____
_____ .

10. The best thing about my writing is _____
_____
_____
_____ .

11. The step in the writing process I most need to improve is _____
_____
_____
_____ .

12. I need to work on this because _____
_____
_____
_____ .

Name _____ Date _____

Peer Conferencing Notes: Reader

Directions: Read your classmate's draft and make suggestions for improvement. Remember that your classmate needs specific suggestions. Ask yourself one or more of these questions, make notes on your answers, and share your answers with the writer.

Name of Writer _____ Date _____

Name of Reviewer _____ Date _____

1. What do you see as the writer's purpose? Is it clear?

_____

_____

_____

2. Is the topic too broad/too narrow to cover in a paper like this? If so, how should the writer narrow/broaden the topic?

_____

_____

_____

3. Does the beginning make me want to read the rest of the paper? If not, why?

_____

_____

_____

4. Are there places where you wish the writer had included more information? If so, where?

_____

_____

_____

5. Are there parts that could be left out? What are they?

_____

_____

6. Are there places where the writer could have used more exact or appropriate words? What words do you suggest?

_____

_____

7. Are the ideas presented logically and are they easy to follow? Are there any parts you found confusing? If so, what parts?

_____

_____

_____

8. What could the writer do to make the paper easier to follow?

_____

_____

_____

9. What do you like best about the paper? Why?

_____

_____

_____

_____

_____

_____

10. What one thing could the writer do to most improve this paper?

_____

_____

_____

Proofreading Checklist

Directions: Use this checklist to review the grammar, usage, mechanics, and spelling before presenting your work. You may want to use the proofreading symbols shown here to mark your draft. It is usually best to first make any revisions in organization, detail, transitions, and similar elements.

Proofreading Marks

Mark	Meaning	Mark	Meaning
∧	Insert a letter or word here.	#	Insert a space here.
⊓n\t⊔	Switch the order of two letters or words.	¶	Begin a new paragraph.
✗	Make this letter lowercase.	≡	Capitalize this letter.
‿	Link inserted material.	∧	Add a comma.
＂ ＂	Add quotation marks.	⊙	Add a period.
ℯ	Take out a word, sentence, or punctuation mark.		

Grammar and Usage

_____ Do the subjects and verbs in my sentences agree?

_____ Did I use complete sentences?

_____ Did I incorrectly run any sentences together without proper punctuation? Have I corrected them?

_____ Did I use the correct form of irregular verbs?

_____ Did I indent the first line of each paragraph?

_____ Did I use the correct form of personal pronouns?

_____ Did I use adjectives and adverbs correctly in comparisons?

_____ Did I use any double negatives? If so, did I correct them?

Punctuation and Capitalization

_____ Did I end each sentence with the correct punctuation?

_____ Did I use commas and semicolons correctly?

_____ Did I capitalize all proper nouns correctly, including names of characters, nicknames, and place names?

_____ Did I begin each sentence or direct quotation with a capital letter?

_____ Did I use quotation marks to show the beginning and end of another's exact words?

_____ Did I use apostrophes where needed to show possession or missing letters?

Spelling

_____ Did I check the spelling of the names of people and places?

_____ Did I use the correct form of words that sound alike but have different spellings and meanings?

_____ Did I check the spelling of words I am not sure of, especially troublesome words like _their_ and _there_?

Organization

_____ Did I make my thesis clear?

_____ Does each paragraph contain a topic sentence?

_____ Did I make sure that the topic sentences support my thesis?

_____ Did I elaborate on my main ideas?

_____ Did I pull everything together in a strong conclusion?

Name _____ Date _____

Writing Self-Assessement

Directions: These questions will help you review the process you used to write a paper. The best time to use this is immediately after you have published or presented the final version, while the experience is still fresh in your mind. You may wish to review your answers to these questions before you write your next paper.

Title of Paper _____

Type of Writing _____

Date Begun _____ Date Completed _____

1. I used the following strategy for choosing and narrowing my topic:

   _____

   _____

2. How successful was this strategy? Would I use it again? How would I change it the next time?

   _____

   _____

3. How did I gather information for this paper? Was this an efficient and productive method? What other method might I have used?

   _____

   _____

   _____

4. How did I decide on the organization for the information I gathered? Was this a good strategy for making that decision? Are there other strategies that might have worked better?

   _____

   _____

   _____

5. The prewriting activities that helped me the most when writing the draft were

   _____

   _____

6. In revising and editing my draft I tried to focus on _____

   _____

   _____

   _____

7. One strategy I used in revising that helped was _____

_____

_____.

8. One strategy I wish I had tried is _____

_____

_____

_____.

9. In proofreading for grammar, usage, mechanics, and spelling errors, I need to pay more attention to

_____

_____

_____

_____

10. The thing I did most successfully in this paper was _____

_____

_____

_____

_____

11. The thing I most need to work on in my next paper is _____

_____

_____

_____

_____.

12. The next time I write a paper of this type, I want to be sure to remember

_____

_____

_____.

Name _____ Date _____

Portfolio Planner

Directions: Use this form to record and clarify the goals of your portfolio and to identify the strategies and resources you expect to use in pursuing those goals. Keep a copy of this planner handy to track your progress and record notes from conferences with your teacher. When your portfolio is complete, use this form in conjunction with the Portfolio Self-Evaluation form to assess how well you did.

Part I: Goals

1. Type of portfolio:

_____ Working Portfolio to collect and organize work in progress

_____ Presentation Portfolio to showcase my best work

_____ Other _____

2. My specific goal for this portfolio is _____

_____

_____

_____

3. To achieve this goal, I will need to focus on developing the following skills:

_____

_____

_____

4. The finished portfolio will show the following things about me:

_____

_____

_____

5. The finished portfolio will demonstrate the following strengths and abilities:

_____

_____

_____

Part II: Strategies and Resources

6. I will need to do these assignments and activities to reach my goals:

_____

_____

_____

7. I expect to complete this portfolio by _____.

8. Complete the following chart to plan the specific steps in completing your portfolio. As you complete each step, record the date in the last column.

Goal:

Step	Task: Assignment or Activity	Materials and Resources Needed	Will Be Completed By	Date Completed
1.				
2.				
3.				
4.				
5.				
6.				
7.				
8.				

Plan Approval

Date of Conference _____ Teacher's Signature _____

Suggestions _____

Progress Check

Date of Conference _____ Teacher's Signature _____

Suggestions _____

Date of Conference _____ Teacher's Signature _____

Suggestions _____

Name _____ Date _____

Portfolio Record

Directions: Use this form to record and update information about the writing you place in your portfolio. You may want to attach this form to the cover of your portfolio so it serves as a reminder to record all contents. Your teacher may ask you to keep a portfolio for a particular unit of study. If so, indicate the unit represented by this portfolio.

Unit _____

Title of Paper _____

Stage of Development: Prewriting   Date _____

                            Drafting   Date _____

                            Revising and Editing   Date _____

                            Finished Paper   Date _____

Title of Paper _____

Stage of Development: Prewriting   Date _____

                            Drafting   Date _____

                            Revising and Editing   Date _____

                            Finished Paper   Date _____

Title of Paper _____

Stage of Development: Prewriting   Date _____

                            Drafting   Date _____

                            Revising and Editing   Date _____

                            Finished Paper   Date _____

Title of Paper _____

Stage of Development: Prewriting   Date _____

                            Drafting   Date _____

                            Revising and Editing   Date _____

                            Finished Paper   Date _____

Title of Paper _____

Stage of Development: Prewriting   Date _____

                        Drafting   Date _____

                        Revising and Editing Date _____

                        Finished Paper   Date _____

Title of Paper _____

Stage of Development: Prewriting   Date _____

                        Drafting   Date _____

                        Revising and Editing Date _____

                        Finished Paper   Date _____

Title of Paper _____

Stage of Development: Prewriting   Date _____

                        Drafting   Date _____

                        Revising and Editing Date _____

                        Finished Paper   Date _____

Title of Paper _____

Stage of Development: Prewriting   Date _____

                        Drafting   Date _____

                        Revising and Editing Date _____

                        Finished Paper   Date _____

Title of Paper _____

Stage of Development: Prewriting   Date _____

                        Drafting   Date _____

                        Revising and Editing Date _____

                        Finished Paper   Date _____

Name _____ Date _____

Portfolio Final Self-Evaluation

Directions: This evaluation form will help you assess your completed portfolio. Review the contents of your portfolio and answer the following questions to see which goals you have met and which goals you need to continue working toward.

1. Does your completed portfolio meet the goals you set for this unit? _____ If your answer is yes, list the items you feel fulfill the goals and explain your choices. If your answer is no, tell why.

   _____

   _____

   _____

   _____

2. Does your completed portfolio satisfactorily demonstrate the strengths and abilities you specified? _____ If your answer is yes, list the items and tell how they demonstrate the strength or ability. If your answer is no, explain why you are not satisfied that this strength or ability has been demonstrated.

   _____

   _____

   _____

3. Which step in your planning chart was completed most successfully? What made this step successful? Which step proved to be the most difficult? What made this step difficult?

   _____

   _____

   _____

4. The best thing about the work in this portfolio is _____

   _____

   _____.

5. The most important thing I learned in completing this portfolio is _____

   _____

   _____.

6. The thing I am least satisfied about in this portfolio is _____

   _____.

7. A goal for my next portfolio will be _____

   _____.

Name _____ Date _____

Portfolio Final Evaluation: Teacher Rating

Directions: Use this form for an overall assessment of the completed student portfolio. In addition, you may ask the student to complete a Portfolio Final Self-Evaluation form. These forms can be placed in the portfolio and referred to during student or parent conferences.

I. Assessment of Individual Items

Rate each item in the portfolio from 1 to 4, with 4 being the highest.

Item and Goal	Rating	Comments

II. Overall Assessment

Rate the overall achievement of the portfolio in these areas using the following rubrics:

_____ Focus

  4. All items reflect a clear sense of goals and a focused strategy for attaining them.

  3. Most items reflect the stated goals of the portfolios, but work includes a few unproductive strategies.

  2. Goals are lacking in clarity, and strategies have regular lapses in focus.

  1. No consistent goal and generally aimless activities in this portfolio.

_____ Variety

4. Items are highly varied and demonstrate competence and creativity in many areas.

3. Items reflect some variety and demonstrate competence and creativity in several areas.

2. Items are generally of one type with some new competencies and/or occasional creativity.

1. Items are of one type and show little or no concern for originality.

_____ Attitude

4. Shows enthusiasm for and commitment to achieving stated goals.

3. Generally positive about achieving stated goals but shows occasional periods of inactivity or low interest.

2. Needs regular urging or reminders to complete steps in the portfolio plan.

1. Completely lacking in enthusiasm and commitment; works on portfolio only after repeated reminders.

_____ Progress

4. Portfolio shows substantial progress over previous work in a broad range of skills and competencies.

3. Measurable growth and progress in several areas of skills and competencies.

2. Modest growth and progress in one or two areas.

1. No noticeable growth in any area; work is mechanical and repetitious.

Additional observations: _____

_____

_____

The best work in the portfolio is _____ .

An area needing further attention is _____

_____

_____ .

Some goals for the next portfolio should be _____

_____

_____ .

Evaluator's Signature _____

Date _____

Name _____   Date _____

Self-Assessment: Speech

Directions: When you speak before a group, your goal is to present information to your listeners in an interesting way. When you give a speech, you usually want your words to persuade listeners to believe or do something. Use this sheet to evaluate your speaking techniques and to assess your ability to compose and deliver an effective speech.

Circle the word that best applies to your speaking habits and techniques.

1. I look forward to speaking before a group.   never   occasionally   always

2. I plan what I am going to say before I begin to speak.   never   occasionally   always

3. I speak in a clear, confident voice.   never   occasionally   always

4. I use language and gestures that are appropriate to the occasion, audience, and purpose.   never   occasionally   always

5. I engage listeners by making eye contact.   never   occasionally   always

6. When I have to give a speech, I prepare in the following ways:

   _____ I do the necessary research to speak intelligently on my topic.

   _____ I consider my audience and purpose when choosing anecdotes, facts, details, and quotes to include in my speech.

   _____ I organize my ideas in a way that will be clear to follow.

   _____ I decide on an appropriate opening statement, quotation, joke, or anecdote that will hook listeners.

   _____ I rehearse my speech to improve my performance.

7. I recently gave a speech on _____

   _____.

8. The best part of my speech was _____

   _____.

9. The part that listeners seemed to like the best was _____

   _____.

10. If I were to give that speech again, I would make it better by _____

    _____.

Name _____ Date _____

Peer Assessment: Speech

Directions: Use this sheet to assess a speech given by one of your classmates. Be honest but keep in mind that harsh, critical comments can be hurtful. Your goal is to help your classmate recognize the successful elements of his or her speech as well as areas that need improvement.

Name of Speaker: _____

Topic: _____

_____ Assigned by Teacher   _____ Chosen by Student

Rate the speaker according to the following scale. Write the matching number in the space.

Point Scale

4 = Thoroughly   2 = Very little
3 = Mostly   1 = Not at all

_____ **1.** The speaker prepared for this speech.

_____ **2.** The speaker was relaxed and confident.

_____ **3.** The speaker spoke clearly and slowly.

_____ **4.** The speaker made eye contact with listeners.

_____ **5.** The speaker used appropriate gestures and facial expressions.

_____ **6.** The speaker used graphic aids effectively.

Use your own words to assess each element of the speech:

Introduction _____

_____

Body _____

_____

Conclusion _____

_____

Organization of Ideas _____

_____

_____

Sentence Variety _____

_____

Level of Interest _____

_____

Name _____ Date _____

Peer Assessment: Oral Interpretation

Directions: A successful oral interpretation communicates the message of a piece of literature. Read the guidelines for a successful presentation of an oral interpretation and use them in two ways:

1. Follow them as you prepare an oral interpretation.

2. Use them to evaluate others' interpretations.

As you listen to a classmate's oral interpretation, write your assessment of how the speaker meets each guideline.

Speaker's Name _____

The oral reading was taken from _____.

Oral Interpretation Guidelines	Your Assessment of the Speaker
1. The piece of literature is selected with the audience and a specific purpose in mind. The time allowed for the presentation is considered.	
2. The work is cut, but the order of the story events still remains clear. Speech tags (*she smiled*) that can be presented through body language can be cut. Passages that do not contribute to the dramatic effect the speaker hopes to achieve can also be cut or trimmed.	
3. The introduction gives the title and author of the work and sets the scene for the part of the story that will be read. Any important events that took place earlier in the story are included.	
4. The speaker uses his or her face, body, and voice (volume, pitch, tone, pronunciation, speed) to build drama, bring the characters to life, and create an overall impression.	
5. The speaker allows the audience time to react to humorous, surprising, sad, or other emotional parts of the reading.	

Peer Assessment: Dramatic Performance

Directions: You may have an opportunity to watch two or three of your classmates give a short dramatic performance. Use this sheet to evaluate their performance. Answer each question as thoroughly and as honestly as you can.

1. Who participated in the performance? _____

2. What work did they perform? _____

3. How appropriate was the work for the audience? _____
   _____

4. How prepared were the student performers? Did they know their lines?
   _____
   _____

5. Were the movements, gestures, and facial expressions appropriate to the work? Explain.
   _____
   _____

6. How well could you hear the performers? Why do you think this was so?
   _____
   _____

7. Did the performers make use of any props during the performance? In what way did they enhance or detract from the performance?
   _____
   _____

8. How did the audience react? _____

9. Overall, I think this performance was _____
   _____.

10. If students have a chance to perform this work again, I would suggest they
    _____
    _____.

Name _____ Date _____

Self-Assessment: Listening

Directions: Active listening is an important part of the learning experience. Use this sheet when you listen in school to help you evaluate your success as an active listener.

Put a check mark next to each statement that applies to you.

Listening Skills	Always	Sometimes	Seldom	Never
1. I am relaxed and attentive.				
2. I determine the speaker's purpose and my purpose for listening.				
3. I think about what the speaker is saying and recognize the main points.				
4. I am polite. I do not interrupt or cause any kind of disturbance.				
5. I concentrate on the words, especially toward the middle of the presentation when I might tend to become distracted.				
6. I ask questions whenever I do not understand something.				
7. I take notes when appropriate.				
8. At the end of an oral presentation, I mentally summarize what I have heard.				
9. In a discussion, I allow others the chance to speak.				
10. In a discussion, I listen carefully to a speaker so that I can respond appropriately.				

11. What do you think are the most important traits of an active listener?

_____ _____

_____ _____

12. Which of the traits that you listed is your strongest? Which is your weakest? What can you do to improve that trait to become a better listener?

_____

_____

Name _____

Date _____

Self-Assessment: Speaking and Listening Progress

Directions: This page is designed to help you track your speaking and listening progress. This chart will give you insight into your average daily speaking and listening opportunities.

Rating Key   E = Excellent   G = Good   S = Satisfactory   NI = Needs Improvement

Date	Place	Speaking/Listening	Describe What Happened	Rating

Name _____

Date _____

Speaking Progress Chart: Teacher Observation

Directions: This chart is designed to help you assess your students' speaking behavior. Write the students' names in the first column. Use the key to record your observations for each behavior. Share your observations with students to help them recognize their speaking skills and to help them set goals for improving.

Key   **P** = Proficient   **I** = Improving   **N** = Needs Attention

Student's Name	Speaks clearly and loudly.	Appears calm and confident.	Is prepared and knows material.	Uses body language and gestures effectively.	Uses visual aids effectively.

Name _____ Date _____

Teacher Observation Checklist

Directions: This instrument is designed to help you identify and record behavior related to future job performance. It has been derived from a report by the Secretary's Commission on Achieving Necessary Skills (SCANS) published by the Department of Labor. In the center column, write a brief description of the behavior observed and the date and circumstances of the observation. In the right column indicate the level of readiness you assess this behavior demonstrates: **P** for Preparatory, **W** for Work Ready, and **A** for Advanced. Add to this log periodically throughout the school year.

I. Basic Skills: Reading	Behavior	Level of Readiness
1. Locates, understands, and interprets written information from text, graphs, or schedules to perform a task.		
2. Identifies the main idea or essential message in written text.		
3. Infers relevant details, facts, and specifications.		
4. Uses contextual clues or finds meaning for unknown or technical vocabulary.		
5. Judges the accuracy, appropriateness, style, and plausibility of reports or proposals of other writers.		
II. Basic Skills: Writing		
6. Records information completely and accurately.		
7. Uses graphs and flowcharts to present information.		
8. Uses language, style, organization, and format appropriate to the subject matter, purpose, and audience.		
9. Includes supporting documentation.		
10. Uses appropriate level of detail.		
11. Checks, edits, and revises for correct information, appropriate emphasis, and form.		
12. Checks, edits, and revises for correct grammar, spelling, and punctuation.		

III. Basic Skills: Listening	Behavior	Level of Readiness
13. Critically evalutates a verbal message.		
14. Responds appropriately to a verbal message.		
15. Critically evaluates nonverbal messages, such as body language.		
16. Responds appropriately to a nonverbal message.		
IV. Basic Skills: Speaking		
17. Communicates oral messages appropriate to listeners and situations.		
18. Makes a positive contribution to conversations and discussions.		
19. Makes a positive contribution to a group presentation.		
20. Selects an appropriate medium for conveying a message.		
21. Uses language appropriate in style, tone, and level of complexity to the audience, the message, and the occasion.		
22. Uses body language appropriate to the audience, the message, and the occasion.		
23. Articulates a message clearly and confidently.		
24. Understands and responds to listener feedback.		
25. Asks questions when needed.		
V. Thinking Skills: Creative Thinking		
26. Uses imagination freely.		
27. Combines information in new ways.		
28. Makes connections between seemingly unrelated ideas.		
29. Revises goals in ways that reveal new possibilities.		

VI. Thinking Skills: Decision Making	Behavior	Level of Readiness
30. Specifies goals and limitations.		
31. Generates alternatives.		
32. Considers risks.		
33. Evaluates and chooses best alternatives.		
VII. Thinking Skills: Problem Solving		
34. Recognizes that a problem exists (i.e., identifies a discrepancy between what is and what should or could be).		
35. Identifies possible reasons for discrepancy.		
36. Devises and implements a plan to resolve discrepancy.		
37. Evaluates and monitors progress of the resolution.		
38. Revises plan as indicated by findings.		
VIII. Thinking Skills: Reasoning		
39. Uses logic to draw conclusions from available information.		
40. Extracts rules or principles from a set of objects or written text.		
41. Applies rules and principles to a new situation.		
42. Determines which conclusions are correct when given a set of facts and a set of conclusions.		

Date _____

Dear Parent or Guardian,

Recent studies show how important parental involvement is in helping students achieve success in school. Because I know that you want your child to have an excellent year in English, I am pleased to tell you about our curriculum and suggest some ways you can participate in improving your child's performance.

In English this year we will be using *Prentice Hall Literature: Penguin Edition.* This program combines a wide variety of quality reading selections with literature analysis, critical thinking and reading skills, and composition. Importantly, it connects the literature to students' own experiences through the development of themes relevant to students' lives.

You can help your child get the most from this program and from all of his or her homework by following this expert-tested advice.

- **Find the best time for studying.** Work with your child to decide on the best time for studying. Then set that time aside at least five days out of every week. If there is no homework, your child can use the time to review or plan ahead.

- **Eliminate common distractions.** Set aside a study area that is free from noise and other distractions. Turn off the TV. Your child may say that watching television is helpful, but no research supports this. In fact, watching television allows students to turn off their minds because it requires no action or interaction.

- **Avoid common interruptions.** Take messages if the telephone rings and have your child alert his or her friends not to drop by during the established study time.

- **Provide physical conditions that help concentration.** Ensure that the study area has adequate lighting and is kept at a comfortable temperature. Provide a table or desk that has enough space for writing.

- **Keep supplies handy.** Keeping studying materials nearby saves time. Placing them in a small bucket or box makes it easy to move them to the study area. A list of supplies should also include a dictionary and a thesaurus.

- **Encourage computer literacy.** Help your child to see the value of using the computer to write his or her compositions and other assignments. Encourage your child to use the computers at school or the public library. If you have a home computer, provide quality word-processing software for your child.

- **Ask to see your child's books.** Looking through the books gives you a better idea of what your child is learning and shows him or her that you think the material is important.

- **Ask to see your child's work on a regular basis.** You do not need to criticize or regrade the papers. That will only make your child less willing to show you his or her work. Just let your child know you are interested.

- **Read.** By watching you read, your child will see reading as a valuable activity. You can be especially effective if you occasionally read and discuss one of the selections your child is covering in class.

I look forward to working with your child and hope you will contact me if you have any questions during the school year.

Cordially,

_____

English Teacher

Name _____ Date _____

Self-Assessment: Home Review

Directions: Fill in the name of an adult friend or family member on the line below and attach the completed *Initial Self-Assessment.* Plan to spend some time discussing your writing with this person. You will not be asked to turn in this page. It is entirely between you and your friend or family member.

Dear _____,

    We are about to begin our work in writing at school. I used the attached self-assessment page to help me think about the types of writing I have done, to examine how I go about the task of writing, to analyze my strengths and weaknesses, and to set goals for the year.

    I would appreciate if you would look over my answers and goals and review them with me from time to time. I will share some of the things I write in school with you so we can both follow my progress.

    In addition, I would be interested in knowing something about your experiences with writing. For example,

1. What kinds of writing have you had to do? How important was it that you wrote well in those situations?

2. How and where did you learn to write?

3. What are your strengths and weaknesses as a writer?

4. Do you think writing will always be an important skill? Why?

_____

_____

_____

_____

_____

                               Sincerely,

Name _____ Date _____

Homework Log

Directions: Use this homework log to keep track of your daily assignments. After completing each assignment, have a parent or guardian look over your work and sign the log.

Subject and Assignment	Date Due	Date Completed	Parent/Guardian Signature

General Resources

Name _____ Date _____

Writing: Home Review Letter

To the Student: Fill in the name of a family member or an adult friend and attach this letter to the final version of your work to request comments on your work.

Date _____

Dear _____,

    I am attaching something that I wrote in school recently. I would appreciate it if you would read it and tell me what you think of it. I am particularly interested in getting your answers to the questions below. You can answer them on the lines under each question.

What do you think my purpose is for writing this?

_____

Were you able to follow my thoughts? If not, where did you get lost? What could I have done to make it easier to follow along?

_____

Is there any information you wish I had included? If so, what?

_____

_____

Are there any parts you think I could have left out? If so, which parts?

_____

_____

What do you like best about what I have written?

_____

_____

What else would you like to tell me about what I have written?

_____

_____

    Thank you for your help.

Sincerely yours,

_____

Writing Student